SEARCH
FOR
REALITY

SEARCH FOR REALITY

PSYCHOLOGY
AND THE CHRISTIAN

GARY COLLINS

KEY PUBLISHERS

Wheaton, Illinois 60187

TABLE OF CONTENTS

To Julie

FOREWORD

Here is a thoroughly evangelical study of the religious
and spiritual aspects of psychology. Dr. Collins openly
avows his own commitment, taking Scripture as divinely authoritative. He therefore confesses his belief
in the reality of the supernatural — miracles, redemp-
tion, faith-healing, conversion and demonology. At the
same time, however, he has not produced one more
tract camouflaged as a piece of scholarship. He has
produced, instead, a work which is impressively fair,
balanced, and objective. He refuses to endorse the
uncritical, streamlined explanations which are prevalent in some Biblically-oriented circles — e.g., all emotional disturbance is attributable to an individual's sin;
psychology and Christianity are irreconcilable enemies;
every valid answer to personality needs and problems
is to be found only in the Word of God. With a candor
that matches his commitment, Dr. Collins points out
the complexity of issues that are often viewed much
too superficially by his fellow-believers. As one of his
fellow-believers, I therefore greatly appreciate his refusal to engage in pious over-statement, together with

his insistence on exploring the neuroticism and kookishness, as he calls it, which may accompany doctrinal
orthodoxy.

I appreciate, too, his lucidity, his skill in making
difficult terms and ideas understandably simple. He
takes intricate subjects and succeeds in rendering them
shiningly intelligible to people who might otherwise
dismiss psychology as an occult mystery.

I appreciate, also, his practicality as he shows the
relevance of theory and research for the Sunday School,
the pastoral ministry as well as for self-understanding.
Thus when he talks about B. F. Skinner, he includes
several pages which illustrate the possible application
of new learning techniques to Bible study. The seem-
ingly abstruse becomes surprisingly pertinent.

But all of this is done, I must emphasize, with a
breadth of knowledge, a grasp of contemporary developments, and an unobtrusive use of the significant literature which will elicit the respect of readers who
disagree with Dr. Collins' convictions and conclusions.

In short, this is the sort of book evangelicals have
needed for years. It will serve as an antidote to misconceptions which spuriously claim Biblical sanction.
Hence, both negatively and positively, it will render
the cause of Biblical Christianity a valuable service.

— Dr. Vernon C. Grounds

PREFACE

The purpose of this book is to provide an introduction to the modern science of psychology as it relates to the Bible and the work of the church. It has not been written for professional psychologists or for those who have a broad understanding of the science of psychology. While such readers might be interested in the encounter between psychology and Christianity, it is likely that they will find parts of the book elementary. This could be especially true where psychological terms are defined or well-known research is described. The book will be of great interest to Christian laymen, church workers, and students who are interested in relating the science of psychology to the Christian faith.

A number of people read and critically evaluated earlier drafts of the manuscript. I am especially grateful for the thoughtful and sometimes painfully honest comments of Dr. Richard Lovelace, Dr. James Johnson, and the psychology majors in the 1968 graduating class at Bethel College, St. Paul, Minnesota. I also appreciate the efforts of Sandra Rowe, Diane Edlund, Timothy Babbage and Mrs. Theodora Barrett who deciphered my writing and laboriously typed the various revisions. Finally I want to thank my wife for an encouragement and patience which is always present, but which was especially in evidence during the weeks when I worked on this manuscript. Her relevant comments and suggestions concerning grammar are reflected in almost all of the following pages. It is to her that this volume is lovingly dedicated.

G. R. C.

1

INTRODUCTION

The period of history in which we live has been given a number of labels. Ours has been called the space age, the age of science, the technological age, the age of anxiety, and the age of psychology. The latter term gained wide acceptance when it was used in a series of articles which appeared in *Life* magazine several years ago. "We live in an age of psychology," the articles stated.

The new science of human behavior has, within a few decades, changed the nature of modern life. . . . Its findings . . . have pervaded our lives, subtly changed our thinking, our actions, and our language. . . . Practically anything relating to psychology and psychiatry finds a big audience. . . . Books of psychology or psychiatry for the layman often become best sellers. . . . All indications are that the expansion of psychology and psychiatry up to now — as spectacular as it has been — is only . . . beginning.[1]

Since the above was written, the author's predictions have been clearly supported. The growing influence of psychology is reflected in the number of professional psychologists (the American Psychological Association now has over 25,000 members), the increasing number of high school and college level courses dealing with this subject, and the emergence of psychology in such diverse places as hospitals, clinics, factories, advertising companies, prisons, schools, businesses, government agencies, military installations, churches, and seminaries.

That psychology has become a significant influence in churches and seminaries is interesting when one considers the history of psychology. For many years psychologists either ignored or were critical of religion. Sigmund Freud, for example, stated that religious doctrines were all illusions and that religion was a group neurosis. He hoped that mankind could overcome this unhealthy dependence on religion as science progressed and as society matured. In the years following Freud, other psychologists described religion as a crutch for emotionally unstable people who could not face their problems alone. Still others ignored religion entirely, believing that it is non-scientific and thus beyond the realm of psychological study. As might be expected, many Christians reacted to these attitudes with distrust and criticism of psychology.

Happily these attitudes have begun to change during the past couple of decades. There has been a more friendly interaction between at least some groups within the church and some branches of psychology. This is the result of a shift both in the church's attitude toward psychology and in the attitudes of many psychologists toward religion.

In 1925 a minister named Anton Boisen was hospitalized as a mental patient. Following his release from the hospital, Boisen established a summer internship program which gave theology students the opportunity of working with mental patients in a state hospital. From modest beginnings such as this, a field known as "pastoral psychology" developed which today plays an important role in the training of seminary students and clergymen. Pastoral psychology examines the insights, findings and methods of psychology, and seeks to determine which of these has relevance and applicability to the work of the pastor and church.

While the pastoral psychology movement has been developing within the church, a number of psychologists have begun to take a second look at religion. They are coming to recognize that the spiritual influences in a person's life cannot be explained away or ignored. Thus, some of the most significant books dealing with the integration of psychology and religion have been written by past presidents of the American Psychological Association.[2]

In the pages which follow, an attempt will be made to show how modern psychology relates to the truths of the Bible and the work of the church. Before progressing any further, two issues should be discussed: the meaning of psychology and the author's views of scripture.

Psychology can be defined as a science, and an art, which studies the directly observable behavior of men and animals and the less directly observable feelings, thoughts, motives, and self-concepts that cause or accompany such behavior. The purpose of psychology is to understand, predict, and control the behavior of men and animals. Psychology is a science because it attempts to apply rigid scientific techniques — in so far as this is possible — to the study of behavior. The psychologist is concerned with behavior which is directly observable — such as a man's actions or words — and with the behavior which is less easily seen — such as a man's feelings and thoughts. While psychology is primarily a science, it might also be defined as an art which involves the skillful application of psychological principles to the individual problems of people who are having difficulty in their personal adjustment, in their marriages, with their schoolwork, or with their businesses. Both in the scientific laboratory and in applied situations, psychologists attempt to understand, predict, and control behavior. Although psychologists are interested in the behavior of both men and animals, in this book we will focus attention primarily on the psychology of human behavior.

The Bible, of course, is viewed differently by its many readers. At one extreme we have those people who seem to believe that the entire Bible was dictated by God and that every word in our current English versions is God-given. At the opposite extreme are those who feel that the Bible is an interesting old book of literature which contains wise sayings and delightful myths but which is in no way a revelation from God. In any book dealing with the Bible and science the reader has a right to know where the author stands in his view of scripture. It is this writer's view that the Bible, both the Old and the New Testaments, is God's verbal revelation to men. While parts of the Bible were dictated (most notably the Ten Commandments and parts of the Revelation) most of the Bible was given to us by God through the writings of committed, Spirit-controlled men. In ways unknown to us, these holy men were inspired by God to write in their own style the messages which were a direct revelation from God.[3] As originally written, in their original languages, the words of scripture were without error. During the course of numerous translations, it is conceivable that some errors may have crept into the Bible. It is the author's personal belief, however, that a God who revealed himself to men, through nature, through the scripture and through His Son would not permit the written Word of God to be distorted by translators. Therefore, the Bible, as we now have it, is the Word of God and can be understood as such by any believer who takes the time to study it, guided by the Holy Spirit.

The Bible and contemporary psychology both tell us something about man. The Bible shows us what God has revealed about man and the science of psychology teaches us what man has discovered about himself and his behavior. As the revealed Word of God, the Bible is able to shed light on the science that seeks to understand, predict, and control human behavior. But the Bible is not a scientific textbook! It does not use scientific terms, and it makes no attempt to explain events from a scientific point of view. Since psychology *is* a science, psychology can contribute to our understanding of human behavior and of the events described in scripture.

In the chapters which follow we will consider some of the topics that are dealt with both in the pages of scripture and in the writings of modern psychology. We will attempt to discover where psychology and the Bible are in agreement and in disagreement, and we will suggest some ways in which the disagreements might be resolved.

In proceeding with this study, we must recognize that there will be times when the words of scripture and the findings of psychology will appear to be so much in contradiction that at present there can be no integration. Dr. Paul Meehl, a distinguished psychologist and a past president of the American Psychological Association has summarized the way in which a Christian must handle these kinds of problems.

He takes it for granted that revelation cannot genuinely contradict any truths about man or the world which is discoverable by other means (including science). If such appears to have happened, he must operate on the assumption that this is only an appearance. That being presupposed, he then seeks to resolve the contradiction. ... If the resolution cannot be effected, the problem is put on the shelf as a mystery, not solvable by the lights of nature or of grace but only by the light of glory.[4]

[1] *Ernest Havemann,* The Age of Psychology, *New York: Simon and Schuster, 1957. Quotations are taken from the back cover and from pages 7, 8, and 20.*

[2] *Notable books on religion by past A.P.A. presidents have included Gordon W. Allport,* The Individual and His Religion, *New York, MacMillan, 1950; Paul E. Meehl, et. al.,* What, Then, is Man? *St. Louis: Concordia, 1958; and O. Hobart Mowrer,* The Crisis in Psychiatry and Religion, *Princeton, New Jersey: Van Nostrand, 1961.*

[3] *II Peter 1:21.*

[4] *Paul Meehl, et. al.,* What Then, is Man? *p. 181. Reproduced by permission of Concordia Publishing House.*

2

PSYCHOLOGY AS A SCIENCE

All science proceeds on at least two basic assumptions. First, science assumes that the world contains facts and events which can be accurately observed. In the scientific literature these facts are called *observables,* since this is what the scientist observes, or *variables,* since the scientist tries to vary these facts when he conducts his experiments. The second assumption is that these facts are organized and related to one another in consistent and lawful ways. It's the two-fold purpose of science to observe facts as accurately as possible and to discover ways in which the facts are related to each other.

Let us illustrate this with a simple example. Assume that tonight, before going to bed, a man decides to give his dog fresh water. At ten o'clock in the evening the man places a dish of water on the back porch. On his way into the house he notices that the thermometer reads 42 degrees Fahrenheit. The next morning, as he is leaving for work at 7 A.M., the man notices that the thermometer reads 27 degrees Fahrenheit and that the dog's dish is filled with ice. One does not have to be a scientist in order to realize what has happened to the substance in the dish. During the night the temperature has dropped below freezing and the water has frozen. For the sake of discussion, however, let us assume that we have never known water to freeze and that we want to study this occurrence by using the assumptions and methods of science.

The scientist has *observed* six facts. On one occasion he has observed the water, the 42 degree temperature, and the ten o'clock reading on the clock. On another occasion he has observed the ice, the 27 degree temperature, and the hands on the clock pointing to seven. Since he assumes that facts are in some way related, the scientist would carefully conduct an experiment in order to determine whether there is any *relationship* between the change in the substance in the dish, the differences in the readings of his thermometer, and the change in the positions of the hands on the clock. It might be noticed that the scientist has observed the substance in the dish without the aid of instruments, while the temperature and the time have been measured with instruments known as a thermometer and a clock.

After conducting his experiments, (and repeating the procedure several times so that he is sure of the results) the scientist could conclude that water will solidify whenever it is left for a period of time in a temperature which is below 32 degrees Fahrenheit, and when there is no variation in other factors such as water movement. Whenever the temperature is below freezing, water changes into ice.

Conclusions such as these are known as laws or principles of science. During the course of history, scientists have discovered a number of laws to account for the events that take place in our world. Discovery of such laws is important because once they are known, it is possible to control our environment. Once he discovered the laws concerning the influence of temperature on water, man was able to make ice cubes and brew hot tea. Once man discovered some of the laws which account for the growth of plants, he was able to increase agricultural production and grow more robust African violets in his living room. When man discovered laws to account for chemical reactions, he was able to manufacture aspirins and other drugs, develop new techniques in medicine, and create a host of labor-saving devices. Thus, by assuming that the observed facts of science are related in an orderly manner, scientists have uncovered a number of laws which have enabled man to make fantastic technological advances.

Psychology as a Science

Like any other scientist, the psychologist wants to accurately observe facts and to determine how the facts are related. Eventually, psychologists hope to discover laws or principles which will explain why people behave as they do.

Sometimes it is possible to get accurate observations of behavior by casually watching people and animals as they go about their daily activities. This kind of observation is not very precise. Two people observing the same event are likely to see things differently. Furthermore, as our definition of psychology would indicate, psychologists are interested in more than observable behavior. They are concerned about the less directly observable feelings, thoughts, motives, and self-concepts that accompany behavior. Since these cannot be seen accurately by casual observation, tests and other instruments have been developed which permit more precise measurement. Frequently such careful observations are made in psychological laboratories. By conducting experiments both within the laboratory and without, psychologists have been able to arrive at a number of conclusions regarding the ways in which facts are related. These conclusions are being formed into laws of behavior.

Determinism and Revelation

Thus far we have seen that science believes in an orderly world where nature functions in accordance with a number of principles or laws. Psychological scientists believe that behavior is orderly and that men act in accordance with certain principles or laws. From this we can see why almost all scientists — including psychologists — believe in *determinism*. This is the assumption that all events in the world are caused or determined by some preceding event. As the natural scientist works on the assumption that nature exhibits regularities and that the events of nature are caused, so the psychologist assumes that behavior exhibits regularities and that the behavior of men is caused. In making his observations, conducting his experiments, and seeking to discover scientific laws, the scientist is really seeking to discover what it is that determines or causes the events or behavior that he observes.

Does the assumption of determinism contradict scripture? One psychologist has suggested that this deterministic view, which is accepted so readily by contemporary scientists, is the "strongest intellectual enemy of the church and among educated people gives the most powerful no to the churches' proclamation."[1] If all human behavior is determined and explainable by the laws which psychological science seeks to discover, then there would appear to be no place in psychology for miracles, for the intervention of God in people's lives, or for man's free will.

In discussing this problem, Meehl gives an interesting appraisal of how the determinist would account for Paul's conversion.

According to the determinist his (Paul's) experience and behavior as described in Acts 9:1-9 must all conform to the laws of psychology and physiology.... If we imagine a super-psychologist who knew all these laws of the mental life and who possessed an exhaustive knowledge of Paul's precise psycho-physical state and of the incoming stimuli at the instant of his conversion, the determinist thesis asserts that this imagined psychologist could have predicted the conversion with all its particulars.[2]

In other words, according to the determinist position, every event that happened to Paul on the road to Damascus should be explainable in terms of the laws of science.

The person who believes that the Bible is divine revelation, might pass off this deterministic description of Paul's conversion as sheer nonsense. Surely, it might be argued, the light which came from heaven, the voice which was heard by Paul and the men in his party, the subsequent blindness, and the tremendous change in Paul's life can hardly be explained by the natural laws of human behavior. In addition, there appear to be many other events in the Bible which defy naturalistic explanation. Consider, for example, the day when the sun stood still while the children of Israel completed a battle,[3] the virgin birth of Christ, the raising of Lazarus from the dead, and — what is undoubtedly the most significant event in all of the New Testament — the resurrection of Christ. Do these events show that scientific determinism and scriptural revelation are at odds and unable to find a common meeting ground? Must we conclude that there is no place in science (including psychology) for those people who accept the Word of God?

The Christian psychologist, because he is a psychologist and a scientist, must assume that behavior is orderly, lawful, and determined. If he is a Christian, the psychologist must also accept the fact that God can and does intervene in the affairs of men, and that man has some free will to determine his own destiny. Indeed, he must believe that the Christian is of all men most free.[4]

The conflict between determinism and the truth of divine revelation can only partially be resolved. Since the Bible is not a scientific textbook, it does not tell us anything about the physics, physiology, or psychology of events such as Paul's conversion or other apparent supernatural happenings. It is possible that God intervenes in the affairs of men by working through the natural laws which He has created, which He sustains, and which He permits science to discover. Perhaps all of the events in scripture which we now consider to be supernatural will someday be explained by naturalistic principles. This in no way limits the divine intervention of God in the affairs of men. We can believe both that behavior is determined according to established laws and that God influences men through these principles. However, it is also possible to accept the belief that while most behavior is determined, *some* events are the direct result of divine supernatural intervention and can never be explainable by natural laws. If this is so, then the task of the psychologist is to uncover the scientific laws which explain *most* of behavior.

The question of human freedom and scientific determinism has been debated by philosophers for centuries. It is the old problem of man's free will and the sovereignty of God. While there appear to be scriptural references to support both positions, this is basically a difficult theological and philosophical issue which is beyond the scope of this book.[5]

While neither the Christian nor the non-believer will be very satisfied with the conclusions reached in this debate, the whole question of scientific determinism and the revelation of God leaves us with the following:

1. Determinism is a working assumption which has enabled science to progress. A belief in determinism has lead to the discovery of principles which have enabled man to gain significant control over his world. While it may not account for all behavior, determinism is a useful hypothesis that we would be foolish to reject.

2. Individual freedom and responsibility is another useful assumption which guides the behavior of most men and appears to be consistent with divine revelation.[6]

3. The influence of God in the affairs of men is also a truth which is revealed in scripture[7] and which must be accepted by faith because it is beyond the realm of scientific inquiry. In spite of this scientific impasse, which has stumped the finest of philosophers and theologians for centuries, science has progressed and Christians have continued to believe in and experience the hand of God in the lives of men.

[1] *Paul Meehl, et. al.,* What, Then, is Man? *St. Louis: Con-Concordia Publishing House, 1958, p. 173. Reproduced by permission.*

[2] Ibid., *p. 176.*

[3] *Joshua 10:12, 13.*

[4] *John 8:36; Galatians 5:1.*

[5] *For a further discussion of these issues, see Chapter 9.*

[6] *Job 19:4; Ezekiel 18:20; John 3:15-18; Romans 2:1-16; 14:12; Galatians 6:5.*

[7] *Genesis 45:8; Proverbs 16:9; Acts 4:27-28; Romans 8:28-29; 9:20; Ephesians 1:10-11; II Timothy 1:8-9.*

3

THE NATURE OF MAN

What is man? Many years ago the Psalmist asked this question[1] and for centuries since, theologians and philosophers have turned to scripture and to their own speculative reasoning in an attempt to describe human nature and to say what man is really like. The nature of man is not a question which interests only theologians and philosophers. Recently a distinguished American psychologist suggested that "people today are asking more urgently than ever before, *what sort of creature is man?*"[2]

It should not be surprising that this question concerns psychologists. When they conduct research into human behavior, when they attempt to understand the causes of normal and abnormal activity, and when they engage in psychotherapy, psychologists are guided by their views of man's nature. If we view man as being primarily a biological animal, we will treat him differently than we will if man is considered to be a divinely created individual who is capable of free will. If a therapist believes that man is innately good and capable of planning his own future, the treatment may differ significantly from that of a therapist who believes that man is a mechanical robot whose behavior is mostly determined by environmental events.

In attempting to discuss human nature as understood by psychology and as revealed in scripture we encounter two problems. First, neither psychology nor theology has a clear statement about the nature of man. Psychologists hold a number of views on this topic and these various opinions may account for the different research emphases and techniques of therapy. Likewise, Christians — even those who accept the authority of scripture — have different ideas of what man is really like. Thus we cannot contrast *a psychological* view of man with *a Biblical view*. Instead, we must see how psychological views contrast with Biblical and theological views.

A second problem which is encountered in a discussion such as this concerns language. Psychology is a science attempting to use precisely defined scientific terms. The Bible, on the other hand, is not a scientific volume and uses terms which are much more difficult to define with precision. Words like "ego," "emotion," and "depression" are psychological terms which do not have clear parallels in scriptural language. On the other hand, words like "mind," "soul," or "spirit" are Biblical terms which are psychologically meaningless. For this reason, when we attempt to make "abnormal behavior" equal to "sin," or when we liken Freud's "id" to "man's sinful nature" we are likely to be inaccurate and often misleading.[3] This is similar to a Frenchman and an Englishman communicating with each other in their native tongues. Communication and mutual understanding is, at best, limited.

In spite of these two difficulties, we will attempt in this chapter to give some of the more commonly held psychological views of man, make statements about the

Biblical views of man, and attempt to determine if these are in any way related.

Psychological Views of Man

While there are many existing opinions about man's nature, both within the field of psychology and without, we will limit our consideration to five of the more commonly held viewpoints.

The Mechanical View of Man

Sometimes called "the naturalistic view," suggests that man is a physical being who reacts to the events in his environment like a typewriter would react to fingers pounding on the keys. Every action of man, every joy and sorrow, every desire, results from an external influence which leads the individual to "react." The psychologist who accepts this view (and this means most American psychologists including those who are known as "behaviorists") is interested in knowing how humans respond when they are stimulated. Abnormal behavior is thought to be the result of some stimulation which leads to inefficiency. Therapy consists of treating the individual like one would deal with a plant or laboratory animal. If we provide the right stimulation, this view holds, the individual will change. Within recent years there has been an attempt to liken man to a big computer who is "fed information" from the environment, processes the information, stores some of it in his memory "system" and makes responses.

While many people might object to the reduction of human beings to the level of a machine, this approach has stimulated a tremendous amount of research. It has taught us much about human behavior and, as we shall see in subsequent chapters, it has led to significant advances in both teaching techniques and in the treatment of abnormal behavior. While we do not like to think of ourselves as robots, it must be recognized that in many respects man *is* like a machine responding to the stimulation that comes from the environment.

The Biological View of Man

Closely related to the mechanical view is the position that man is primarily a complex biological animal. Undoubtedly he is the best developed of the animals but he is still a physiological specimen whose primary function is survival and reproduction. Darwin held this position and it was pretty much accepted by Freud. The biological view of man's nature probably gave impetus to much of the psychological interest in animals. If man is an animal, it was concluded, why not study simpler biological organisms with the hope that we can acquire knowledge that will apply to complex human animals? Some psychologists have even created "experimental neurosis" in dogs and cats, and then developed treatment techniques for these animals in order to determine if this sheds light on the causes and treatment of abnormal behavior in human beings.

It cannot be denied that the biological viewpoint has led to a greatly increased understanding of human behavior. Man, of course, *is* a biological organism. In some respects he does act like the pigeons and white rats which psychologists so often study, and even those neurotic cats and dogs have given us some good clues about human behavior.

We normally do not think of a plant or animal as being good or bad. Likewise, most psychologists who hold the biological viewpoint assume that man is neither good nor evil. Freud, however, was an exception. He believed that man was basically a bad animal. When he is born, Freud believed, man is a collection of impulsive, self-centered, irrational urges. Few modern psychologists would accept this pessimistic description of man, but perhaps this comes closer to Biblical revelation than any other aspect of Freud's theory.

The Culturalistic View of Man

This view states that a man's nature is largely molded by the society in which he is raised. To understand man, we must understand the social forces by which he has been influenced. Abnormal behavior is seen as a failure to meet cultural expectations, and the goal of therapy is to encourage the individual to adjust or adapt to the group norms.

This view recognizes the significant role that society plays in contributing to individual behavior. It is undoubtedly true that our religious beliefs and forms of worship are dependent on the beliefs and ways in which our parents and teachers worshipped.[4] Few people in North America offer sacrifices to stone gods and I would guess that people in primitive areas do not sing gospel songs in tall buildings with stained glass windows.

If we accept the culturalistic view we must conclude that there is no external standard of behavior for man. The only "right" is what our particular society considers to be right. Certain sexual behaviors which would be considered immoral in our culture, might be all right in another society. Such a view is, of course, strongly opposed to the teaching of scripture where God has standards of right and wrong which go beyond culture. In addition to this moral objection, the culturalistic view of man leaves little room for individuality. It would seem to suggest that as an individual develops, he must give up his uniqueness and conform to the social mold.

The Humanistic View of Man

Within recent years a number of psychologists have criticized those who attempt to reduce man to the level of a machine, an animal, or a social mold. It has been suggested that man is much more complex and responsible than these descriptions. Humanism, is an example of a viewpoint which regards man as basically good, rational, self-sufficient, able to control his own future, to solve his own problems, and to realize his unique potentialities. Research is designed to study man's creativity and capabilities. It is assumed that the person who experiences emotional problems is not meeting his capabilities and the goal of treatment is to provide an environment where man can solve his own problems. Dr. Carl Rogers has expressed this view quite clearly. He believes that man is *not* fundamentally hostile, anti-social, destructive, or evil. Instead, he believes that man is characteristically good, positive, forward moving, constructive, realistic, and trustworthy.[5]

Is man as rational and capable as humanists would have us to believe? The Bible does not present man in such a good light and even our own experiences might lead us to conclude that the humanists paint an unrealistically positive picture of human nature.

The Existential View of Man

Existentialism has no single answer to the question of what man is like. Some existentialists, for example, say that man is useless, while others claim that he is a valuable creature who is related in some way to God.[6] All would agree, however, that man is something more than a machine or an animal.

According to this viewpoint, if we are to understand man, we must know how he feels, how he experiences life, and how he views the world around him. From these deliberations the existentialists have concluded that man is basically restless, anxious, insecure, and struggling to find meaning in life. The existential therapist hopes that man will somehow be able to overcome this depressing state and find some purpose in his existence.

Like the others, this viewpoint has increased our understanding of human behavior and contributed to the psychologist's treatment techniques. Undoubtedly existentialism has most clearly described one of the significant and widespread discontents in our society — lack of meaning and purpose in life.

But is man basically hopeless? Must we view life from such a pessimistic and despairing point of view? Many Christians would be inclined to answer "no."

Undoubtedly all of these views have helped psychologists to advance their science towards the goal of understanding, predicting, and controlling human behavior. Men do respond to their environment like machines. We are animals and our behavior is largely molded by the society in which we live. As the most capable of living creatures man has made significant advances and appears to have real worth. But man is also a creature of feeling who is seeking to find meaning to life. Even this composite view, however, falls short in giving an accurate description of the true nature of man. Psychology cannot completely understand normal and abnormal behavior and psychologists cannot fully appreciate how behavior can be altered, without investigating the Biblical statements about man.

Biblical Views of Man

While theologians and Bible scholars are not in complete agreement concerning a Biblical view of man's nature, all agree that scripture says a great deal about the problem. The Bible gives us at least eight facts about the nature of man. Some of these agree with current psychological thinking while others are clearly in disagreement.

Men Are Created

Man is a being who was created by God.[7] While the Bible does not go into great detail regarding the method God used in the act of creation, we do know that man was formed from the dust of the ground, that he was given life by God, that he was good in his original state, and that his continued existence depends on both the will of the Father and the power of the Son. God recognized that man would be lonely by himself, so woman was created to provide fellowship and to be man's helper.[8]

Men Are Unique

While man is certainly a biological organism, and while he does react to the influences of his culture and environment, the scriptures give man a unique place in the universe. Man is unique in at least four overlapping ways.

First, man was created in God's image or likeness.[9] What does this mean? Obviously, since God is a spirit, the resemblance which man bears to God cannot be something physical. Some theologians have concluded that perhaps man has "a spark of divinity" but such a belief has little support from scripture. The context of the phrase "in the image of God" suggests that the reference is to the preeminence of man over the world in which he has been placed. This brings us to the second unique characteristic of man.

Man is the most superior creature in the world. God gave man dominion over everything that had been created on the earth.[10] It is little wonder that science has been able to have such control over the world of nature. Usually this is attributed to the progress of man, but scripture would suggest that man makes this progress because God has given the ability.

Thirdly, man is rational. Obviously he can think, retain knowledge, and consciously experience emotion. But this does not put man in a unique category among created beings. There is psychological evidence to show that animals can also retain knowledge, engage in simple thinking, and experience emotion. Man, however, was also given the ability to make moral choices and to use language. This does put him in a unique category above all other creatures on earth.

Finally, man is unique because he is a spiritual being. The term "spirit" is one of these theological terms which is difficult to define and has no psychological equivalent. Nevertheless, this characteristic of man is something which apparently has not been given to the animals but is unique to human beings.[11]

Men Are Equal

While a few contemporary psychologists have asserted that some men are better than others, this is not supported by scripture. In a very dramatic vision, God showed Peter that all men are of equal significance and there are a number of Bible passages which support this conclusion. Of course, men differ in their appearance, personality traits, education, and cultural background but these differences are not significant in God's sight.[12]

Men Are Valuable

The scriptures teach that man is a creature of worth. When he was created, man was given glory and honor and put in a position which was just a little lower than heavenly beings. God valued man and loved him so

4

CHRISTIANITY: A CRUTCH FOR THE UNSTABLE?

When I was an undergraduate in college, taking my first course in psychology, our class was required to make several visits to a local mental hospital. I can still remember my surprise at seeing so many evidences of evangelical Christianity. Many of the patients had Bibles. There were hymn books on the ward piano similar to those which were used in my home church. Many of the patients talked like evangelicals, expressing concern about their "sin" and their need to "be saved." Indeed, my first experience with mental patients led me to wonder if state hospitals were populated by Bible-believing Christians.

Although subsequent experience has taught me that this conclusion was wrong, over the years I have met a number of patients who appear to be Christians.

Florence M. was a middle-aged pastor's wife who had been committed to a mental hospital because of extreme depression. She was obviously familiar with scripture and appeared to be a Christian. She complained, however, that she felt "empty inside" and that she had "committed the unpardonable sin." She wanted to commit suicide but reportedly refrained from doing this because of the influence it might have on her family. Although she maintained a strong interest in her Christian beliefs, Florence felt that God could not forgive her, that nothing could be done for her condition, and that she would spend the rest of her life in a mental hospital.

Carol J. was a 45-year-old mother of several teen-age children. Her husband had forsaken her for another woman, and Carol was left with the responsibility of guiding her family through the remainder of their tumultuous teenage years. But the children were becoming disrespectful and rebellious. Carol felt rejected, insecure, and unable to meet the demands of her household. When asked how she was coping with her problems, she replied that she thought about happy days in the past, cried, prayed, and waited for God to help. She was making no practical attempts to deal with this frustrating situation, but instead was using her religious beliefs as an excuse to do nothing.

People like Florence M. or Carol J. sometimes lead professional counselors to conclude that religion is bad. Perhaps, it has been argued, religion encourages patients to do nothing about their problems except to ignore reality hoping for the intervention of a deity. Some psychologists and psychiatrists have thus concluded that religion — including Christianity — is primarily a crutch used by unstable people who lack the inner resources and stamina to stand on their own two feet and face their problems.

That religion is a crutch for emotionally unstable people is not a new idea. Many years ago Karl Marx described religion as an "opiate." Bertrand Russell, the English philosopher, called religion an untrue and harmful disease which was used by people who wanted to feel that they had a kind of elder brother who would stand by them in all of their troubles and disputes.[1]

Russell expected that as science progressed, unstable people would no longer need to look around for imaginary supports or to invent "allies in the sky." Instead, he hoped, we would rely on our own efforts here below to make this world a fit place to live "instead of the sort of place that the churches in all these centuries have made it."[2]

It was a psychologist, Sigmund Freud, who most clearly characterized religion as a crutch for unstable people. In his book, *The Future of an Illusion*, Freud wrote that religious doctrines

... are all illusions, they do not admit of proof, and no one can be compelled to consider them as true or to believe in them ... These (religious) ideas protect man in two directions: against the dangers of nature and fate, and against the evils of human society itself.

Countless people find their one consolation in the doctrines of religion, and only with their help can they endure life ...

Thus religion ... (is) the universal obsessional neurosis of humanity ... The effect of the consolations of religion may be compared to that of a narcotic ... The true believer is in a high degree protected against the danger of certain neurotic afflictions; by accepting the universal neurosis he is spared the task of forming a personal neurosis.[3]

In Freud's thinking potentially neurotic people lean on religion to maintain their personal stability. Like Russell, Freud believed that as science progressed religion would no longer be necessary. "Religion is comparable to a childhood neurosis," he wrote, "and ... (we are) optimistic enough to assume that mankind will overcome this neurotic phase just as so many children grow out of their similar neuroses."[4]

In summary, many critics of religion have suggested,

in all sincerity, that religion in general and Christianity in particular, is a crutch, an opiate, a narcotic, or a mass tranquillizer which is used by weak, uneducated, and emotionally disturbed people. By implication, the individual who is strong, well-informed, and emotionally able to face his problems has no need to lean on some imaginary big brother or theological illusion.

Healthy Reactions to Stress

Before considering these charges, it is important to recognize that everybody has problems! Students grapple with academic difficulties, parents have problems with their children, teenagers cannot understand their parents, husbands and wives sometimes have difficulty in getting along with each other, business and professional men face the threat of competition, many twentieth century people are disturbed by a feeling of emptiness and purposelessness in their lives, most of us at some time become discouraged, and only a select few are free of financial problems.

In meeting the problems and stresses of life we use several kinds of behavior which have been helpful to us in the past. At times we discuss our difficulties with a sympathetic friend. Sometimes we meet a problem by hard work and greater efficiency in our efforts. On occasion we try to get away from a problem, relax for a time, and then come back to tackle it afresh. At other times when we are tense or discouraged, we let off steam by knocking around a little golf ball or having a good cry.

Most introductory textbooks in psychology mention another type of reaction to stress. Known usually as "defense mechanisms," these are ways of thinking which we have all learned to use in order to protect us from anxiety, preserve our self-esteem, and deal with many of the stresses which come both from the environment and from within the unconscious. The defense mechanisms are rarely used deliberately, but more often are unconscious reactions to threatening situations. While psychology textbooks may describe upwards of twenty defense mechanisms, it will suffice if we list only a few of the most common types.

Rationalization is the process of making excuses in an attempt to justify something that we have done or failed to do. A college student who puts away his books and goes to a movie on the night before an important examination may justify his actions by saying that he "needed the relaxation." The Sunday School teacher who watches television Saturday night, gets up late Sunday morning, and because of procrastination fails to study his Sunday School lesson, might make excuses for this lack of preparation by saying that he was "too busy." These excuses are known as rationalizations.

Repression is a tendency to exclude from conscious awareness all those desires, impulses, thoughts, and ideas which are threatening. The musician who plays a sour note during a concert may put the memory of this unpleasant and embarrassing experience out of his mind.

Regression occurs when an adult reacts to stress in a way which was successfully used to avoid unpleasant situations at an earlier stage in life. I once had a student who complained of sickness whenever an assignment was due. As a child she had avoided the pressures of school by claiming to be sick whenever there was a test. This technique had worked when she was younger, so she continued to use it in hopes that it would work again now that she was an adult.

Displacement is a defense mechanism which usually occurs when we have been frustrated in some way. Instead of directing our feelings toward the source of the frustration, we direct our feelings toward some other person or object. A few years ago *Post* magazine had a delightful cover showing four pictures. In the first picture a man was obviously being bawled out by his boss. In the second picture the man was shown bawling out his wife. In the third picture the wife was yelling at their little boy, and in the fourth picture the child was shaking his fist at the cat. This is a good example of displacement. The husband was probably mad at the boss but for reasons which are obvious this anger could not be shown in the boss's presence. Instead the man took it out on his wife who in turn took it out on the boy who in turn chased after the poor defenseless cat. Sometimes when we are frustrated or angry we direct our hostilities not toward a person but toward some object. Everyone is familiar with the child who is angry with his parents but slams the door or kicks a piece of furniture instead of attacking the source of his frustration. It is wiser — and safer — to kick the furniture!

Projection is the tendency to blame other people for the deficiencies and motives which really are our own. Perhaps this is an example of "passing the buck." College teachers sometimes see this when students do poorly on an examination. Instead of recognizing that the low grade may result from their own inability or lack of preparation, the students would much prefer to place blame on the professor's poor teaching or the textbook's lack of clarity.

Fantasy is a way of avoiding unpleasant situations by withdrawing into some kind of a dream world. Relaxing with a novel, watching a play on television, or daydreaming are fantasy activities which all of us use at some time.

Identification is a tendency to take on the characteristics of other people whom we admire. The young seminary student who is not doing very well in his first attempts at preaching, may unconsciously begin to imitate the characteristics and mannerisms of some preacher whom he admires.

The use of these defense mechanisms is quite normal. These are healthy reactions which all of us use at times to meet the pressures of life.

Embracing a religious belief is another healthy way to meet our problems. This is especially true of Christianity. Jesus told His disciples to come to Him when they were burdened and He would give them rest.[5] In times of confusion He promised that the Holy Spirit would teach and abide with us.[6] In times of trouble He promised peace and the prospect of a future life of security.[7] For the man who is in need, He promised to supply[8] and for the man who wants guidance He promised to lead.[9] In Paul's letter to the Philippians, the Holy Spirit gives us great words of encouragement when we read "never forget the nearness of your Lord. Don't worry over anything whatsoever; tell God every detail of your needs in earnest and thankful prayer, and the peace of God, which transcends human understanding, will keep constant guard over your hearts and minds as they rest in Christ Jesus."[10] Indeed, the scriptures contain a great wealth of promises which believers can call upon and have found to work in times of stress.

Of course, Christianity is more than a gimmick which enables us to meet the stresses of life. It is more than a crutch or lucky charm which we use in emergencies but otherwise ignore. It is more than a handy defense mechanism. As described in the Bible, belief in Christ involves a personal and growing relationship with an individual. It involves a life that can be characterized by love, joy, peace, patience, kindness, goodness, faithfulness, gentleness, and self-control.[11] It may also involve hardships! The followers of Christ must expect to meet frustrations, rebukes, and hindrances similar to those experienced by Jesus Himself. Indeed, Jesus pictured Christianity not as a crutch, but as a cross. Christianity does not produce a problem-free utopia, but it can create a challenging and healthy way of life which involves both frustration and supernatural power to meet frustration.[12] It is unlikely that Marx or Russell or Freud ever knew of this fuller meaning of Christianity. It may be that many believers have likewise never seen this broader and more healthy picture of the Christian life.

Unhealthy Reactions to Stress

There are times when people fail to use healthy techniques for facing stress. For reasons which we shall outline in chapter four, some people show behavior which is abnormal. Their reactions to stress are self-defeating and sometimes these reactions create greater stresses and lead to more problems.

It is interesting to note that much of the behavior shown by emotionally disturbed people is an exaggeration of the normal reactions which we have described above. While it is normal to discuss our problems with friends, it is unhealthy to talk about one's problems all the time with anyone who will listen. While it is normal to meet a problem by hard work and persistent effort, it is unhealthy to drive ourselves to the point of a breakdown. While it is normal to withdraw from a difficult situation every once in a while, it is unhealthy to run away from problems. "Letting off steam" in some way is a healthy reaction, but the person who cries persistently is not showing normal behavior.

Likewise, all of the defense mechanisms, if used excessively, can become unhealthy ways of meeting stress. When rationalization becomes the persistent tendency to make excuses, when repression becomes a refusal to recognize and face the problems of life, when regression becomes childish behavior, when displacement becomes a tendency to blame others for all of our problems, when projection becomes a paranoid suspicion of other people, when fantasy becomes a schizophrenic withdrawal into our own little world, and when identifications become delusions of grandeur so that the individual thinks he is the president of the United States or some other well-known figure, then the normal reactions to stress have become abnormal. In such instances, rather than helping the individual to face his problems, the defense mechanisms have become problems in themselves.

In addition, for some people, religion, including Christianity, is also distorted and misused during times of stress. According to Dr. James A. Knight, a psychiatrist and Methodist minister, the way in which a person uses his religion

is a good barometer of his mental health. My clinical observations have led me to believe that the positive, health-giving qualities of religion are too numerous to mention. Superficial observations by the psychiatrist may lead him to think that religion has been bad for his patient and that his patient has been the recipient of a "bad" religion. This may be true. Yet, more often, his patient has taken a basically healthy religious faith and distorted or modified it to serve the ends of his own psychological problems. If a psychiatrist's only concept of religion is acquired from mentally ill individuals, he could hardly be said to have a valid picture, or be expected to view religion with sympathy or understanding. This is probably what happened to Sigmund Freud, for his description of religion is distorted and highly biased.[13]

There are several ways in which religious teachings

can be distorted by emotionally disturbed people. First, as people are faced with great stress, there are changes in their behavior. They may, for example, show unusual emotional reactions. They may misinterpret the events in their lives or the intentions of other people. Their thinking may become unclear, and in some cases the person may become disoriented so he does not know who or where he is. When the overall thinking of a patient becomes this confused, it is not surprising that his thoughts about religion also become distorted. A counselor who meets with such a patient might correctly conclude that religious ideas are a reflection of the mental illness. From this, some have reached the erroneous conclusion that all of religious experience indicates abnormality.

A second and perhaps more common way in which religion becomes distorted by the emotionally disturbed occurs when religion is grasped as a "last straw." A man who is drowning will clutch at anything which might buoy him up. Obviously he would not be too concerned with the way in which the buoy was constructed. His concern is simply to grasp something which might keep him from sinking further into the enveloping waters. In like manner, many mental patients tend to grasp at religion as a possible source of strength. If they are clinging to Christianity, they may not know anything about the truths of scripture and they may not be particularly interested in getting an accurate picture of what Christianity is all about. Instead, they cling to the rituals, terminology, and traditions which have become associated with Christianity but are not revealed in the Bible. Even a distorted religious view can give the patient hope, and since he now has something in which to believe, it may even give him comfort and solace in the midst of his problems. In this case a form of religion has become a crutch on which the individual leans. This may explain the prevalence of religious objects which I so often encountered during my hospital visits while I was in college. The patients may have been clinging to religious symbols, but probably very few were aware of any Biblically based Christianity.

If psychologists, psychiatrists, and other counselors who work with disturbed individuals get the impression that religion is basically bad, one might ponder the extent to which disturbed people teach distorted and unhealthy interpretations of Christianity to others who are not psychologists. How many children, for example, have developed immature and distorted views of Christianity because of the well-meant, but incorrect, religious views which they have heard from their parents or other adults?

Conclusion

In our daily lives all of us encounter stress. In growing up we have learned that there are certain techniques of behavior which enable us to cope with life's pressures. Most of these techniques are healthy in that they enable us to meet the stress and carry on as efficiently functioning individuals. At times, however, some of us develop reactions to stress which are unhealthy in that they do not solve our problems efficiently, but tend instead to increase or add to the problems. When people persist in using these unhealthy ways of meeting stress, their behavior ceases to be normal.

Religion (which in our western society usually means some form of Christianity) is frequently used by both mentally healthy and emotionally disturbed people to help them meet the pressures of life. Too often, however, those who lean on "Christianity," are embracing a distorted view of scriptural truths. The Bible teaches that Christ came into the world in order that His followers might have a full, meaningful, and abundant life.[14] He expected that we would bring our problems to Him and He promised to meet our needs when the burdens got heavy.[15] Often overlooked, however, are the responsibilities of the individual who would become a follower of Christ. God loves us and has a plan for our lives; but since man is sinful and separated from God,[16] he cannot know and experience God's love and plan for his life. By coming to earth and dying for man, Jesus Christ took care of man's sin and made it possible for us to know of God's love and plans for us.[17] Scripture teaches, however, that we must receive Jesus Christ as Savior and Lord by a personal invitation.[18] Only when we have done this is it possible to experience a new way of living, a new source of divine strength and a superhuman wisdom which enables us to meet the situations of life more effectively.

When these truths of scripture are accepted in a partial or distorted form, professional counselors are encouraged to believe that only emotionally unstable people embrace Christianity. It is assumed that by placing their trust in a Divine Person, committed Christians also demonstrate that they are unstable by nature and unable to meet problems by themselves.

We must acknowledge that a form of Christianity is used as a crutch by emotionally unstable people. We must also recognize that well-adjusted believers "lean on" Christ. But the life which any individual can have in Christ is more than a crutch. It is a cross and a costly form of discipleship. It can also be a source of power and peace, a personal relationship with God Himself, and a meaningful way of living which is superior to every alternative.

[1] *Bertrand Russell*, Why I am Not a Christian. *New York: Simon and Schuster, 1957.*

[2] Ibid. *p. 22.*

[3] *Sigmund Freud*, The Future of an Illusion. *Garden City, New York: Doubleday Anchor Books, 1927. pp. 54, 29, 61, 77-78, 87, 79.*

[4] Ibid. *p. 96.*

[5] *Matthew 11:28-30.*

[6] *John 14:26.*

[7] *John 14:27, 1-3.*

[8] *John 14:13-14.*

[9] *John 14:6; Psalm 32:8; Proverbs 3:5-6.*

[10] *Philippians 4:5-7, J. B. Phillips.*

[11] *Galatians 5:22-23.*

[12] *John 16:33.*

[13] *"The Use and Misuse of Religion by the Emotionally Disturbed." In James A. Knight,* A Psychiatrist looks at Religion and Health. *New York: Abingdon, 1964. p. 85. Used with permission.*

[14] *John 10:10b.*

[15] *Matthew 11:28-30.*

[16] *Romans 3:23.*

[17] *Romans 5:8; John 14:6.*

[18] *John 1:12; Revelation 3:20. The outline of this paragraph is based on the four spiritual laws as presented by Campus Crusade for Christ, Arrowhead Springs, San Bernardino, California 92403. The author is grateful to William R. Bright, President of Campus Crusade for Christ, International, for permission to incorporate this outline into the present chapter.*

5

WHY DO CHRISTIANS CRACK UP?

What happens when a person "cracks up"? What is a "nervous breakdown"? What do we mean by "mental illness"? These questions all refer to the abnormal behavior which often results when people are overwhelmed by the stresses of life.

But what is abnormal behavior? The prefix *ab* means "away from"; thus *ab*normal behavior is that which is away from or different from what is normal. Unfortunately, psychologists and others who have considered this question have been unable to agree upon a definition of what is normal. Because there are differing viewpoints, writers of psychology books usually indicate what they mean by abnormal behavior. In this book, the term "abnormal" will be used in three ways.

1. *A person is abnormal if his behavior is at odds with the social expectations of the society in which he lives.* Among psychologists, this is the most widely used definition of abnormality. The murderer, dope addict, sex deviate, hermit, or hebephrenic who sits by himself and giggles all day, are all acting in ways

which are abnormal. Their behavior is different from what our society expects of normal people.

When we think of abnormal behavior in this way, we must recognize that what is abnormal in one society may be quite normal in some other culture. In the United States and Canada it is normal to be friendly, to laugh, and to appear happy, but it is abnormal to be overly suspicious of all other people. In the Dobu culture of New Guinea, just the opposite is true. Extreme suspicion of one's neighbors is normal but laughter and expressions of happiness are taboo. The thoroughly maladjusted Dobu is the man who is pleasant and naturally friendly.[1]

When abnormality is defined in this way, it can exist for long or short periods of time, and can result from a variety of causes. The hospital patient who is delirious after surgery is showing abnormal behavior but this is relatively short in duration and is probably the result of some well-defined physical cause.

2. *A person is abnormal if he experiences internal conflicts which lead to intense and prolonged feelings of insecurity, anxiety, and/or unhappiness.* Here is the individual who is at odds with himself. He has standards of behavior which he cannot attain, goals in life which he cannot reach, urges which he cannot suppress, fears which he cannot overcome. He may feel insecure, inadequate, or without any purpose in life. He has failed to measure up to the standards which he hopes to meet. While such persons are well-meaning and want to do right, they stand condemned in their own eyes and are afraid that they will be rejected by others.[2] Many people are able to hide their ever present conflicts and show behavior which is socially appropriate; others may be so distracted by these inner tensions that they act in ways which people consider to be odd or unusual.

Such inner turmoil is, to a large extent, culturally based. A child does not inherit inner tension. He must learn to be insecure, anxious, or unhappy, and such learning must come from his society. The things which cause us to worry may be very different from the things which bother some African tribesman. The issues which are of concern to a business man may differ greatly from the tensions that face a busy mother and housewife. The problems of suburban white men differ from the frustrations of black men in the ghettos.

At times, of course, all of us experience internal conflict, insecurity, anxiety, and unhappiness. Almost all men strive to improve behavior, attain goals, and overcome fears. If we were satisfied with ourselves and our behavior, there would be no growth toward maturity. A person is considered abnormal, not when he experiences internal tensions, but when the tensions are intense, prolonged, and usually incapacitatory.

3. *A person is abnormal if he is separated or away from God.* Although man was created in God's image, he rebelled and was forced to leave the garden where he had been in communication with the Father.[3] But it is not normal for man to be separated from God. He needs to be close to his Creator. Since man is unable, by his own efforts, to re-establish this closeness, a Divine provision was made which permits anyone to return to God.[4] We are returned to a state of oneness with the Creator when we acknowledge our sinful separation from God, believe in the resurrection of Jesus Christ, and invite Him to be Lord of our lives.[5] This is normal. It is a truth which applies to all men, regardless of cultural background.

Most modern textbooks in psychology would accept the first two of these definitions of abnormality, but few would accept the third. All three are important and it is unlikely that a man can really be at peace with society and self, until he is at peace with God. By defining abnormality in three ways we are suggesting that it is very rare and perhaps impossible for a person to be completely normal: at peace with his society, at peace with himself, and at peace with God.

Abnormality in Christians

There is a tendency among many Christians to assume that all abnormal behavior is caused by spiritual problems. A "nervous breakdown" in a Christian is regarded as a sign of spiritual weakness, and it is assumed that those who walk in a close relationship with God will never experience mental illness.

At first glance there appears to be strong evidence in favor of such a view. Persons with emotional difficulties are often characterized by fear, worry, confusion, discouragement and loneliness. These are all topics with which the Bible deals. Since "perfect love casts out fear" the Christian has no need to be fearful.[6] Philippians 4:6, 7 would indicate that good Christians should not worry. Verses such as Psalms 32:8 or Proverbs 3:5, 6 show that God leads and thus by implication confusion should not be necessary. Then, with Christ as our constant companion[7] how can a believer be lonely or discouraged?

In spite of these verses there is evidence that sincere Christians *do* "crack-up." Even godly pastors, dedicated missionaries, and devoted church members experience the emotional turmoil which sends them to mental hospitals or to the offices of psychologists and psychiatrists. Here is an example of apparent contradiction between the Bible and our personal experiences. To understand the causes of mental illness in Christians (as well as in non-believers) we must look both to psychology and to scripture.

Causes of Abnormal Behavior

The causes of abnormality are varied and highly complex. Every year psychologists, psychiatrists, and other professionals devote long hours to research projects and careful discussions aimed at finding the precise reasons for abnormal behavior. In attempting to discuss this topic in a few paragraphs we must of necessity reduce a complicated subject into overly simplified terms.

To begin with, it might be helpful to make reference to an old saying — "that's the straw that breaks the camel's back." The break in this situation can be attributed to two conditions. In the first place there is the load which was presumably placed on the animal's back at some time in the past. Perhaps the camel has been weighted down like this on many previous occasions and has developed a strong back which enables him to carry a substantial burden. Since this weight has been placed on the camel at some earlier time it could be said that the load represents the *past influences* on the animal. The second condition which contributes to the "break" is the additional weight of the straw. This might be called the *present stress*. If we were veterinarians attempting to understand why the camel's back broke, we would have to consider both the weight of the past and the stress of the present.

At the risk of pushing this illustration too far, let us make some guesses about other ways in which the camel's back could be broken. In the above illustration the weight of past influences was heavy and the present stress was light. The camel's back would also break if to a light load of past influences there was suddenly added a very heavy present stress. Dropping a load of cement on a camel that was only bearing a saddle would surely cause a break. It would also be important to consider the build of the camel. Some camels may be very strong and able to bear heavy weights and heavy stresses, while other camels may be weaklings with backs that would break under relatively light weights and mild stresses.

In considering the reasons for psychological "breakdowns" in people, it is important to consider both past influences and present stresses. For some people the past has not contributed to good mental health. These people carry such a heavy load of adverse past experiences that a relatively light stress might cause a breakdown. For other people, past influences and previous activities have contributed to emotional stability. They can handle amounts of stress and probably will not "break" unless the present pressures were exceptionally heavy. Obviously there are individual differences in people — just like there are in camels. An event or stimulus which may cause a breakdown in one person may not cause a breakdown in somebody else. Briefly, therefore, let us consider some of the past influences and present stresses which can lead to abnormal behavior. These are summarized in table 4-1.

Past Influences

Physical, psychological, social, and spiritual influences can all contribute to the likelihood of a person developing an abnormality. Let us begin with the *physical* influences. The individual's physique, facial features, temperament, intellectual potential, and body build are all inherited and only partially influenced by the environment. These inherited characteristics can greatly influence how one will respond to stress. The person who is physically weak may react quite differently from the person who is physically strong. The mentally retarded child may have a lower tolerance for stress than does the intellectually normal child.

Many years ago Sigmund Freud pointed out that the

PAST INFLUENCES

- **Physical Influences**
  inherited characteristics
  illness

- **Psychological Influences**
  early upbringing
      lack of love and attention
      rejection
      overprotection
      over-indulgence
      rigid upbringing
  family disharmony
  traumatic experiences
  inadequate learning

- **Social Influences**
  occupation
  social class
  race
  minority group membership
  place of residence
  sex
  marital status

- **Spiritual Influences**
  lack of belief
  lack of meaning to life
  misconceptions about
      Christianity

PRESENT STRESS

- **Physical Stress**
  infection and disease
  brain damage
  drugs
  biological deprivation
      lack of sleep
      lack of proper diet
      lack of oxygen, etc.

- **Psychological Stress**
  frustration
  conflicts
  external pressure

- **Social Stress**
  national events
  war
  economic depression
  civilian catastrophe

- **Spiritual Stress**
  conviction of sin
  guilt
  dissension in the church

INDIVIDUAL

Table 4-1. Causes of Abnormal Behavior: Past influences and present stress both influence the individual. If strong enough, these conditions in combination can result in a breakdown.

psychological experiences which we have in childhood may influence our ability to withstand pressure in later life. It has been found, for example, that little children who do not get love and attention from adults, feel frustrated, insecure, and anxious. Their development is slow, and when they do grow up they are much less capable of handling stress than are people who have had a lot of love in childhood. Psychologists have also shown that young people who are rejected, overprotected, given whatever they want regardless of how unreasonable the request, or placed under exceptionally strict and rigid rules often develop a low ability to withstand stress.

Other harmful early influences include frequent fighting or dissension in the family, and traumatic experiences — such as the loss of a loved one, the observation of a bad accident, or the experience of some frightening event or unexpected danger. Traumatic experiences like these can leave all of us temporarily tense but for some persons the shock is so great that a more permanent insecurity follows. Some people who survive serious automobile accidents, for example, are nervous and highly sensitive for many years.

Finally, there is the psychological influence of inadequate learning. To a very large extent normal behavior is the result of learning. The clothes we wear, the language we use, the way in which we worship, the eating utensils we use, the specific foods we like, and how we get along in social situations are all the result of past learning. Sometimes, however, we do not learn how to meet the stresses and pressures of life. Many people feel very inadequate in social situations because they do not know what to say or have never learned how to get along comfortably with others. High school students experience uncertainty, insecurity, and feelings of rejection if they have never learned how to act on a date. When the pressures of school become intense, college students sometimes panic and become anxious because they have never learned how to study or how to organize their time. In each of these examples, the individual is ill-prepared to face the stresses of life because of inadequate prior learning.

Sociologists and anthropologists have contributed much to our understanding of *social* influences on behavior. Some occupations, for example, place such great pressure on an individual that he is more likely to crack up when new stress comes along. In like manner the social class of a person, his race, his membership in minority groups, his place of residence, his sex, and his marital status, all have a bearing on how he will react to stress.

It is also likely that past *spiritual* experiences can determine our reaction to stress. During the Second World War Dr. Viktor E. Frankl, an Austrian psychiatrist, was held for several years in a Nazi prison camp. As he observed his fellow prisoners, Frankl discovered that the people who most quickly gave up the struggle to live were those who had found no meaning to life, had no reason to live, and lacked faith in the future. In contrast, the prisoners who felt that there was some meaning to life, who were willing to help others, who had something in which to believe, who could appreciate the beauties of nature (even if only in the form of a sunset viewed through a crack in the wall), and who could see some purpose for the suffering — these were the people who maintained psychological stability in spite of their intense discomfort. Frankl is not a Christian, but he recognized that when an individual embraces some kind of faith there is a resulting increase in his ability to withstand stress.[8] Frankl and many of his followers would agree that a person who has expressed faith in a religious, political, economic, or other system, is better able to cope with stress than is the individual who has faith in nothing.

As Christians we believe that faith in the Christ of the scriptures is superior to all other belief systems. When Christ and the Holy Spirit are invited to take control of a life, the individual develops qualities of love, joy, peace, patience, kindness, goodness, faithfulness, gentleness, and self-control.[9] There is a change in his values and an assurance of eternal life to be spent with Christ. This gives our very existence a meaning which need not be shaken by death or suffering. As a Christian, for example, the Apostle Paul found life and death to be equally attractive.[10] Of course, the existence of this God of the Bible cannot be proven scientifically, logically, or psychologically. He is revealed in scripture and must be experienced to be known. Belief in Christ does not necessarily protect us from psychological breakdowns, but such belief does increase our ability to withstand pressure and cope with stress.

Present Stress

Just as past influences can be broken down into four categories, so present stresses can be physical, psychological, social, or spiritual. *Physical* stresses include infections or disease, brain damage, the influence of drugs, and what we might call biological deprivation. The person who is deprived of a balanced diet or sufficient rest, for example, places his physical system under stress. A few years ago a couple of radio announcers decided to hold a contest to determine who could stay awake for the longer period of time. At the end of $168\frac{1}{2}$ hours during which the contestants went without sleep (at which time the attending physician terminated the contest and declared a tie), many signs of abnormality were observed, some of which persisted for weeks after the contest. It is not surprising that people develop mental illness when they permit their bodies to come under excessive physical stress.

When the individual is frustrated, faced with some conflict, or under a great deal of pressure from his environment, he is experiencing *psychological* stress which might cause a breakdown. A *social* stress which most of us experienced in 1963 was the news of the assassination of President John F. Kennedy. At that time, I was employed in the counseling center of a state university on the west coast. The news of the President's death was such a shock to several of our students that they had to be hospitalized. Kennedy's assassination was an international incident but it brought stress to the lives of individuals, many of whom had never even seen or voted for the President. When a country declares war, when there is an economic crisis, or when some civilian catastrophe occurs, environmental forces place tremendous stress on individuals.

Finally there are *spiritual* stresses. Psychological abnormality may result when an individual becomes convicted about some sin in his life or when he is overcome by a sense of guilt. Perhaps this is what happened to King Nebuchadnezzar who, when he became aware of his sin, behaved like an animal.[11] Even tension in the church might be thought of as a spiritual stress. Strife between disagreeing factions is always stressful for the participants. When a church or denomination splits and both sides claim to be following the will of God, the tension is particularly acute and could be too great a stress for some members.

Why Christians Crack Up

By this time it should be apparent that there are

many reasons to account for mental illness. While Christians are "new creatures in Christ" they are still human beings and as such are susceptible to the influences which we have described above. It is incorrect to believe that Christians — even those who are in close fellowship with the Lord — can never develop a psychological abnormality. There are at least six reasons why followers of Christ can and do crack up. The first three of these are unique to Christians. The last three influence the believer by virtue of his being a human being and a member of contemporary society. In considering the following paragraphs it is well to keep in mind the threefold definition of abnormality presented earlier in this chapter.

1. It cannot be denied that for many Christians the cause of their abnormality is strictly spiritual. When a Christian deliberately sins, when he refuses to be controlled by the Holy Spirit, when he neglects prayer and Bible study, when he ceases to trust in God and leans instead on his own capabilities, when he retains habits of behavior which are inconsistent with the teachings of scripture, then it may be that God in his wisdom permits a psychological abnormality to develop. In such cases the abnormality appears to have come as a direct result of rejecting or ignoring God. Such people might be considered abnormal by any or all three parts of our definition of abnormality.

2. There are a number of Bible verses to show that the Lord sometimes permits believers to experience problems in order to produce patience, humility, and a deeper dependence on God.[12] Those whom the Lord loves, He sometimes chastises and the scripture describes such people as "blessed."[13] It is well known that God permitted Satan to bring misery into Job's life, and Paul had a thorn in the flesh from which God never gave deliverance. If the Lord uses such physical

means to increase our spiritual stature, couldn't He also permit mental illness to enter a life to accomplish the same purpose?

While the Lord may permit stresses to enter our lives because He loves us and wants us to grow spiritually, I Corinthians 10:13 would suggest that these pressures would never become intense enough to lead to a severe breakdown. "Every temptation that has come your way is the kind that normally comes to people. For God keeps His promise, and He will not allow you to be tempted beyond your power to resist; but at the same time you are tempted He will give you the strength to endure it, and so provide you with a way out."[14] Psychologist Paul Meehl suggests that this verse applies only to conscious temptations and says nothing about unconscious stress.

The most sanctified Christian may very well carry within him unconscious lusts, fears, or hatreds more than sufficient to create and maintain a neurosis . . . I Corinthians 10:13 cannot be applied in contradiction to this, because that passage treats not of unconscious motivations but of temptations to actual sins.[15]

Probably we cannot dismiss this difficult verse of scripture so easily. The message of the verse is supported by several other scriptural passages which indicate that the Lord will deliver committed believers from the trials and temptations which they encounter.[16] That some people might be delivered into a psychosis is possible but not very convincing. It may be, instead, that God permits some Christians to become psychotic in order that loved ones and other believers might grow in faith. Paul's physical trials increased the faith of fellow believers and it is conceivable that psychological trials could accomplish the same purpose. Perhaps it is wisest at this point to conclude in all humility that as finite creatures who are unable to understand the mind of God, we cannot be sure why committed Christians are permitted to experience the trials and temptations which cause them to crack up.

3. When we think of abnormality in terms of actions which are incompatible with the norms of society, it may be that a Christian who is walking close to God will always appear abnormal to his contemporaries. When Paul told of his beliefs in the court of King Agrippa, Festus cried out that Paul must be mad.[17] On the day of Pentecost, the people in Jerusalem concluded that the disciples were acting so strangely that they were probably drunk.[18] Even Jesus was considered mad by his contemporaries and several modern writers have considered the possibility that Jesus was a paranoid schizophrenic.[19] The Christian who attempts to follow the values and the norms of behavior that are outlined in scripture must by definition act in some ways which are incompatible with the norms and values of western society. When scripture says that we should not lay up for ourselves treasures on earth it is suggesting a guideline that goes against the society's belief in the importance of acquiring material goods. If we love our enemies, as scripture instructs, we are sometimes laughed at by a society which believes that enemies should be hated. A sex-obsessed and pleasure loving society has no place for a philosophy which says we should not make provision for the flesh to fulfill the lust thereof. Nor is our society particularly impressed with a system of values that says we should let no corrupt communication proceed out of our mouths, trust in the Lord rather than leaning on our understanding, or refuse to boast about our plans or accomplishments.[20]

4. Even if we attempt to live in accordance with the

principles of scripture, we are still members of a society. If our society is abnormal and "sick" then we as individuals must be abnormal. Erich Fromm, in suggesting that our society is unhealthy, has listed the delight which we seem to take in war; the development of a whole economy based on the buildup of armaments; the increase of alcoholism, homicide and murder; and the tendency for men to amuse themselves by watching "trash" on television. To this we might add the decline of morals; the rejection of God; the lawlessness and slaughter on our highways; the prevalence of race riots, civil disobedience, union violence and crime; and breakdown in the effectiveness of our law courts. "The fact that millions of people share the same vices does not make these vices virtues." Fromm wrote, "the fact that they share so many errors does not make the errors to be truths, and the fact that millions of people share the same forms of mental pathology does not make these people sane."[21]

5. The Christian, like other people in his society, can experience the early trauma, ineffective learning, or early family disharmony which might lead to insecurity, a poor opinion of oneself, and a lowered ability to withstand stress in later life. Regardless of our beliefs, these unhealthy early tendencies can make us susceptible to subsequent behavior abnormality.

6. Finally, we must remember that many behavior deviations are caused by physical malfunctioning. There is nothing in scripture to suggest that Christians do not experience brain tumors, brain injuries, or brain deterioration. All of these physical influences can lead to behavior abnormality and it may be that in some cases — for reasons described in (2) above or for reasons which we do not understand — Christians develop physical illness with a corresponding mental breakdown.

physical body an unpleasant place for the demons to reside. The famous witch burnings in the middle ages resulted from a belief in demons. It was assumed that burning the demon-possessed was really a blessing to the victims because it freed them from the misery of being in the devil's clutches.

In the 1500's some voices were raised against these cruel tortures and in 1665 an Englishman named Reginald Scot wrote a scholarly attack on demonology. A few years later belief in demons was disappearing and by the middle of the eighteenth century widespread acceptance of demonology was gone. Today almost all psychologists hold the view that demon possession was a belief of ignorant superstitious people, that belief in demon possession is a thing of the past, and that only the most narrow-minded and poorly informed individual would believe that demons exist and influence people today.

Biblical Views of Demon Possession

The Bible makes a number of references to demons. On the basis of these scriptural passages it is possible to reach at least three basic conclusions: demons exist, their characteristics can be identified, and they can be controlled.

The existence of demons. Although the Old Testament makes no direct reference to demons, there are several indications that devils existed and were worshipped by some people.[1] Satan, who is pictured in the book of Job as the chief opponent of God and man, is described as going to and fro throughout the earth creating problems for man, and standing up against God's children.[2]

In the New Testament there are many references to the existence of demons and evil spirits. Jesus believed in demons.[3] The seventy disciples whom Jesus appointed encountered the opposition of demons. The apostles believed in demons, and so did Paul and members of the early church.[4]

The characteristics of demons. According to scripture, demons are spiritual. This means that they are not tangible flesh and blood objects like men.[5] They are evil[6] and have the power to cause harm to men. Scripture points out, for example, that inability to talk, blindness, convulsions, self-mutilation, screaming, and fierce aggressive behavior can all be caused by demons.[7]

The Control of demons. Several times in the New Testament there is evidence that the evil spirits recognized and spoke to Jesus.[8] In spite of their tremendous power, Jesus was able to control them and so were a number of His followers who cast out demons in the name of Christ.[9]

Current Views of Demon Possession

When they consider the historical beliefs in demon possession and the Biblical accounts, most people are inclined to accept one of two current viewpoints.

The first of these states that demon possession is a superstition. According to this view, it is important for us to consider the historical situation and religious beliefs which prevailed during Bible times. Demon possession was widely accepted throughout the whole period in which the Bible was being written. It is also probable that the influence of evil spirits was a common explanation for behavior which at that time was not well understood. Perhaps, this view holds, even the New Testament writers were so steeped in the superstition of their time that they did not recognize that the behavior which they were observing could be explained in a more logical manner. But why did the Son of God believe in demons? Some have suggested that when Jesus took on a human body He also took on a human understanding of current events. As a result, Jesus was influenced by the superstition of his day in the same way as the New Testament writers and disciples. Finally, this viewpoint suggests that much of what scripture explains as demon possession would today be called mental illness, disease, or some form of epilepsy.

The second contemporary viewpoint, and the one with which the author concurs, is that demons did and do exist. While it is true that our interpretations of scripture should remember the historical, geographical, and religious environments of the Bible writers, and while it is true that demon possession apparently was a common explanation for a number of strange behaviors, there is no evidence that Jesus and his disciples were deceived by cultural superstition. Jesus did take on the form of a man, but He is still described as being "the truth"[10] and therefore not deceived by untruthful superstition. On the contrary, Jesus criticized superstition and warned His disciples against it.[11] This being so, it is unlikely that He would have permitted His followers to believe in demons if the existence of such spirits was not real. If Jesus and His disciples were confused about this, we would have to conclude that He was confused about other things reported in scripture, and the authoritative basis of the Bible disappears. Finally, it must be remembered that the demons recognized Jesus. Apparently they knew who He was even before His disciples knew.[12] This, of course, would not be possible if belief in demons was only a result of superstitious thinking.

The Bible supports the idea that people can be indwelt and controlled either by evil spirits or by the Holy Spirit of God.[13] Whether or not the Holy Spirit and a demon can exist in the same body at the same time is a question which is open for debate. On the basis of their personal experiences, some well-known Christians have suggested that such co-habitation is possible. Scripture is the best place to look for an answer, but on this question the Bible appears to be silent. We do know, however, that it is possible for the devil and his forces to direct the behavior of believers, and there are several places in scripture where believers are warned against such satanic influences.[14]

Demon Possession and Mental Illness

If we assume, as the Bible does, that demons exist and influence the behavior of men, does it follow that mental illness is the result of demon possession? The answer to this question is both "yes" and "no." People whom the scriptures described as being demon possessed showed many of the behavior abnormalities which characterize patients in modern mental hospitals. It is certainly possible that some emotionally disturbed patients are actually demon possessed.

The Bible makes a distinction between those who are demon possessed and those who are diseased. While some physical illnesses are attributed to the influence of demons, other diseases seem to come about through natural causes.[15] In like manner the Bible differentiates between demon possession and what we now call mental illness, although in one place this distinction is not clearly maintained.[16]

In this context it is also helpful to look at the experience of missionaries who see more evidence of demon possession in countries where Christ is not widely known. There are enough reports — even by stable, highly educated and well-adjusted missionaries — to suggest that demon possession in foreign peoples is not an isolated event. The following quotation shows not only demon possession in a foreign culture, but points

out that natives differentiate between demon possession
and insanity.

> The demons which people worship are of various orders,
> each with its own name . . . While the air is supposed to
> be full of these terrifying spirits, the water is thought to
> be their special place of abode, reminding one of the spir-
> itual account of that unclean spirit which "walketh
> through dry places, seeking rest and finding none." Many
> other similarities are to be found between the records
> concerning demons in the New Testament and those in
> the life of these backward peoples. I have frequently seen
> natives who are covered from head to foot with scars of
> burning, some unseen power having taken possession of
> them and cast them into the fire. Such occult possession
> is not to be confused with mere dementia. The native rec-
> ognizes the difference between insanity and demon pos-
> session, and calls each by its appropriate name. Actual
> conversation is held by normal people with demons tempo-
> rarily possessing another individual, and the words which
> come from the lips of the possessed are, beyond doubt,
> the words of some other being.[17]

It would be very difficult to carry on a conversation
with a psychotic in the way that normal people described by this missionary converse with demons. Jesus
also conversed with demons in a way which suggests
that demon possessed people were probably not severely
mentally ill.

Demon Possession and Epilepsy

Before concluding this chapter, we should discuss
the theory that demon possession in scripture is really
another name for what we now call epilepsy. Mark 9
records an event which sounds remarkably similar to
an epileptic seizure. "Whenever the demon is in control
of him, it dashes him to the ground and makes him
foam at the mouth and grind his teeth and become

rigid. . . . So they brought the boy, but when he saw Jesus, the demon convulsed the child horribly, and he fell to the ground writhing and foaming at the mouth." The father of the boy then went on to point out that the demon often makes him fall into the fire or into water to kill him.[18]

It is possible that *some* epileptic seizures could be the result of demon possession. However, there is no scriptural, scientific, or logical evidence to support the view that *all* epileptic seizures are caused by demons. Epilepsy is a physical disorder. For some reason, the cells in the brain periodically and temporarily react in a way which sometimes causes the person to be thrown into a convulsion. As with so many physical conditions, epilepsy has been studied by medical science and can be controlled by drugs.

In spite of these facts, people who have epilepsy are often feared and rejected in our society. Could the theory that demon possession and epilepsy are identical, be at the basis of this irrational rejection of epileptics? It must be recognized that epilepsy — like other physical disorders — can strike Christians and non-Christians alike. Some, but not all, epileptic people might be demon-possessed; some, but not all demon-possessed people might be epileptic.

Conclusion

Most modern psychologists, including those who are Christians, attempt to deal with abnormal behavior by using the techniques which we shall outline in chapter 8. Few work on the assumption that their patients are demon possessed, and even fewer attempt to cast out demons. Although most of the deviant behavior and personal problems which we see today probably can be explained by natural causes, this does not eliminate the possibility that some people may be demon possessed. In such cases, scripture would suggest that demons can be cast out in the name of Jesus Christ. Unfortunately, there are sincere Christians who have become so concerned about demonology that they have developed fanciful theories about demons which have no basis in scripture and which distract from the message of the Word of God. While we do not advocate such extremism, no psychologist and no Christian who believes in scripture, should remain ignorant or unalerted to the existence and prevalence of demon possession even in this scientific age.

[1] *Leviticus 17:7; Deuteronomy 32:17; II Chronicles 11:15; Psalm 106:37.*

[2] *Job 1:7; 2:7; I Chronicles 21:1.*

[3] *Matthew 8:28-34; 17:15-18; Mark 5:2-17, are only three of several examples.*

[4] *Luke 10:17; Matthew 17:15-21; Acts 5:16; 8:7; I Timothy 4:1; Acts 16:16-18.*

[5] *Ephesians 6:12.*

[6] *Matthew 10:1; Mark 1:27; Luke 4:36; Acts 8:7.*

[7] *Matthew 9:32; 12:22; 17:15; Mark 5:5; 1:23; Matthew 8:28; Mark 6:3–4; Acts 19:15.*

[8] *Matthew 8:29; Mark 1:24; 5:7; Acts 19:15; James 2:19.*

[9] *Matthew 8:28-34; 9:32-33; 15:22-28; Mark 1:34; 5:2-17; Luke 10:17; Acts 8:7; 16:18; 19:11-12.*

[10] *John 14:6; Ephesians 4:21.*

[11] *Matthew 23:5, 16, 20.*

[12] *While the chronology of the events in Jesus' life is debatable, Mark chapter 1 would suggest that a demon recognized Christ before His disciples knew who He was.*

[13] *John 13:2; Ephesians 5:18.*

[14] *Ephesians 6:11-13; James 4:7.*

[15] *Matthew 9:32-33; 12:22 ;Mark 9:25; 5:5; Luke 13:11 show physical illness that results from demon control. Matthew 4:24; 10:1; 8:16; Mark 16:17, 18 differentiate sickness from demon produced illness.*

[16] *Matthew 4:24; Mark 1:32; Acts 5:16. The exception is Matthew 17:15-18.*

[17] *From Merrill Unger,* Biblical Demonology. *Wheaton, Illinois: Van Kampen, (Second Edition), 1952. p. 89. Quoted by permission of Scripture Press Foundation.*

[18] *Mark 9:18, 19, 22, Living Letters.*

7

NEUROSIS IN THE CHURCH

In the weeks immediately following Christ's ascension, the church on earth was composed of spirit-filled men and women who spent much time in prayer, study, fellowship, and witnessing. They were obedient to the Word of God, willing to share their possessions, and intolerant of dishonesty.[1]

It was not long, however, before dissension began to creep into this company of believers. The Hebrews and the Greeks began to murmur against each other and by the end of Paul's first missionary journey there was arguing and disagreement among the believers. Many of Paul's letters dealt with the unhealthy trends in the church, and when Christ gave his message to the churches in the book of the Revelation, he criticized believers who had left their first love, become fearful, permitted false doctrine, tolerated the presence of ungodly people, had lost their vitality and were smugly self-satisfied.[2]

Within recent years a number of writers have criticized the modern church.[3] Writing in an early issue of *Psychology Today,* Bishop James A. Pike suggested that the church today is like a sinking ship. The church . . .

is listing heavily and water is pouring into the hold. The passengers react in one of three ways: Some ignore the whole thing and keep on playing bridge in the lounge; others rush to help plug the holes and to siphon out enough water so the ship again will be stable and safe; the rest panic, assume the worst, take the lifeboats — and leave the ship.[4]

A number of reasons have been brought forth to account for the problems in the local church, and the tendency for people (especially those who are young) to become church drop-outs. Bishop Pike thought that people are rejecting the church because they think it is "phony". Father Kavanaugh believes that the church is "outdated". Others feel that it is "irrelevant". At the risk of oversimplification, however, I am inclined to agree with a recent writer who suggested that the problems in the church have developed because the membership is no longer centered in the Word of God, but has become centered in man.[5] Over the years church members have built up traditions and unhealthy ways of thinking which have no scriptural basis and which encourage neurosis.

In the next few pages, some of these neurotic tendencies will be considered. It is not my desire to jump on the bandwagon of critics who delight in tearing down the institutional church. This chapter only points out some problems interfering with the fellowship, witness, worship, spiritual growth, education, and benevolent functions that are a vital part of the ministry of the church.

What Is Neurosis?

Before considering neurotic trends in the church, it

would be wise to discuss what is meant by the term "neurosis". Although textbooks of psychology and psychiatry give different definitions of this term, we could conclude that *neurosis is a mild form of abnormal behavior characterized by unhappiness, anxiety, inefficiency, and lack of flexibility.* In addition to these basic symptoms, neurotics have been described as showing conflict between unconscious and conscious motivations or between contradictory desires,[6] inadequacy, high vulnerability to threat, self-centeredness, difficulty in getting along with others, suspicion, lack of insight, irritability, dissatisfaction, impulsivity, guilt, feelings of inferiority, and a number of physical symptoms such as muscle twitches, excessive sweating, heart palpitations, tension headaches, and an assortment of vague aches and pains.[7]

In considering this list two things should be kept in mind. First, not all of these characteristics are found in any one person. Secondly, almost everybody shows some of this behavior at times. Neurosis is so prevalent that one psychologist has likened it to the common cold.[8] It is when the stresses of modern living get too great and the inadequacies from which we all suffer become too strong that neurotic behavior interferes with our efficient functioning.

If neurosis is so common in our society it is hardly surprising that we should find neurotics in the church. When Jesus invited all who were weary and "heavy laden" to come to Him,[9] His invitation surely included those burdened with neurotic characteristics. Christ meets the needs of neurotics and it is right that the body of Christ on earth should receive and help these people. What is discouraging, however, is that this same body of believers frequently acts in ways which accentuate and create neurotic behavior instead of reducing it. Feelings of inferiority, dishonesty, rigidity, disturbed inter-personal relationships, guilt, double-mindedness, and anxiety are all neurotic tendencies in the church which impair our efficiency and create discouragement and unhappiness. Let us consider each of these in greater detail.

Neurotic Trends in the Church

Inferiority and Insecurity

Many years ago a psychiatrist named Alfred Adler, developed a theory in which he stated that everybody feels inferior. Such feelings are unpleasant and lead to tension which must be dealt with by some kind of action. Some people react to their inferiority by complaining. This is a neurotic reaction according to Adler and leads to an "inferiority complex". Such individuals use their felt inferiority as an excuse and a demand for special consideration. Other people react by struggling to overcome their feelings of inferiority in an attempt to feel superior. Might Adler's conclusions apply to many people in the institutional church? Do church members show evidence of inferiority accompanied by complaining or striving for superiority?

Although few of us would care to admit it, church members often demonstrate by their behavior that they are insecure people who feel inferiority and have a low opinion of themselves. As an example we might consider the reluctance of most of us to give a verbal witness of our belief in Jesus Christ. We prefer to be "silent Christians" because we are afraid that someone might laugh if we tell of our faith in Christ. Such behavior surely indicates that we really think the non-Christians' belief is superior. Then there is a hesitancy to live committed Christian lives. We don't want to appear unusual or to behave a little differently lest some non-believers think we are odd. Unconsciously are we assuming that the world's ways are better? We even rationalize our striving for status and material goods by saying that we "want to be attractive" not to alienate anyone who would like to become a Christian. In so doing, we are working on the non-Biblical assumption that men and women are won to Christ because Christians look "sharp" like the world in which they live.

Perhaps an even greater evidence of insecurity in Bible-believing Christians is the emphasis on scripture verses which stress our weakness and inadequacy. The Bible clearly teaches that in his natural state man is a sinner who is alienated from God.[10] However, when we quote Bible verses (often taken out of context) to support the fact that we are weak, inadequate, and worthless, we are really complaining about our inferiority and developing a spiritual inferiority complex. It is possible that we are also concluding that God didn't really improve us when He made us into new creatures.

While some church members complain about their worthlessness (and sometimes develop pride over their supposed humility) others are more likely to react to their insecurity by employing Adler's second solution. If we can strive to be superior and convince ourselves that we are no longer inferior, then, we hope, life will be much more satisfying.

To make ourselves feel superior we commonly use two techniques. First, we talk ourselves into it by repeating over and over again that a Christian is of all men most happy and joyful. As a student I attended a little church where we would periodically have parties. While many of us found these parties rather dull, there was one member of our group who always prayed at the end of the evening and thanked the Lord that "Christians can have as good a time as non-Christians". While this is undoubtedly true, I often wondered if my friend was attempting to convince himself that we really were having a good time and not settling for a poor substitute to the big campus parties. Secondly, church members attempt to be superior by pointing to the inferiority of others both within the church and without. Apparently this is what the Pharisees did when they isolated themselves in smug superiority and looked down on those who did not meet their rigid standards. It may be that this is at the root of the negativism prevalent in the church today. We complacently assume that we alone have the truth and oppose everyone who does not completely agree with our position. Teenagers often find that older church members will not permit open discussion of those practical issues which are not dealt with directly in scripture. The established church members are frequently too insecure to discuss questions such as smoking, social drinking, movies, sex, or dancing. It is easier to generalize, but this is not satisfactory to teenagers, and only helps the established church member maintain his illusion of superiority.

When Christians feel insecure and inadequate but attempt to deal with these feelings by convincing themselves of their superiority, contradictions are bound to result. Sometimes, for example, we are willing to accept incompetence among those who are serving the Lord while at the same time we set impossibly high standards of behavior for our children. Perhaps we accept the incompetence because we realize that all of us feel somewhat inferior. When we set high standards for our sons and daughters we maintain the belief that we really are unusual, superior people.

It is well to recognize that according to the Bible, all men *are* sinners. We have lost the status which God gave to the man which He created. Our righteousness and personal attempts to attain favor in God's sight are worthless.[11] When an individual invites Christ to take control of his life, he becomes a new creature; good in God's sight and valued as a child of God.[12] This does not mean that we immediately stop sinning and become holy and spiritually mature. As we grow in our relationship with Christ, we stumble many times and see our sinful acts in stark contrast to the holiness of God. Still there is no need to complain that we are inferior or to use a lot of artificial devices to convince ourselves and others of our superiority. Because of Christ we have a new relationship with God — a relationship which persists in spite of the pressures, trials, and acts of sin which seem to be characteristic of the growing Christian.

Dishonesty

A few years ago a psychiatrist named Eric Berne wrote a popularly acclaimed book in which he described the games which people play in their relations with each other.[13] These games, according to Dr. Berne, are recurring behaviors which are "superficially plausible" and help us to hide from other people what we are really like. The games are part of a mask behind which most of us hide when we face the world.

Do Christians hide behind masks and play games in their dealings with others? Apparently so. A few years after the appearance of Berne's book a couple of talented Christian writers published a book entitled *Games Christians Play* in which they suggested that even in the church a number of us put up masks to hide what we are really like and to convince other people that we are much more spiritual than we really are.[14]

There are a number of ways in which church members put up a front. Already in the early church there was concern about status. The well-dressed man got better treatment in the worship service than the man

who was poor or shabbily dressed.[15] This awareness
of status continues to the present time. Sociologists
have pointed out that rich people tend to be Episcopa-
lians, Presbyterians, Congregationalists, or Unitarians.
Methodists are one step down in the social scale, followed in order by Lutherans, Baptists, and Pente-
costals.

Even within denominations we see the importance
of status with accompanying power. People who have
been in a church for a long time often have considerable prestige. Christians sometimes put missionaries
at the top of the status hierarchy followed by pastors,
church leaders, and then the "common" members.

While the struggle for status may help us overcome
feelings of inferiority and insecurity, status seeking
is both unscriptural and dishonest. The early church
developed in a culture which had rigid social distinctions, but the apostle Paul pointed out that all Christians are equal.[16] Hiding behind a status mask is a
form of dishonesty and such dishonesty can be psychologically unhealthy.

There is another form of dishonesty which tends to
be prevalent in our churches: spiritual dishonesty.
Most of us pretend that we are growing spiritually and
that we are without spiritual difficulties. In testimony
meetings we talk about the good things that have happened to us and if we mention a sin or problems in our
lives this is usually described as something which happened in the past but is now overcome. Keith Miller,
a layman with a strong appreciation for modern psychology, has given a lucid summary of spiritual dishonesty.

Our churches are filled with people who outwardly
look contented and at peace, but inwardly are crying out
for someone to love them ... just as they are — confused,

frustrated, often frightened, guilty, and often unable to communicate even within their own families. But the *other* people in the church *look* so happy and contented that one seldom has the courage to admit his own deep needs before such a self-sufficient group as the average church meeting appears to be.

Consequently, our modern church is filled with many people who look pure, sound pure, and are inwardly sick of themselves, their weaknesses, their frustration, and the lack of reality around them in the church. Our non-Christian friends feel either "that bunch of nice un-troubled people would never understand my problems;" or the more perceptive pagans who know us socially or professionally feel that we Christians are either grossly protected and ignorant about the human situation or are out-and-out hypocrites who will not confess to sins and weaknesses our pagan friends know intuitively to be universal.

So the new style of life being experienced in the church today begins, I believe, with a new kind of honesty — an honesty which *believes* that *all* of us have sinned and fallen short of the glory of God.[17]

In this paragraph we have a hint of a trend which is gaining enthusiastic reception both within the church and within clinical psychology. This is the tendency to be honest about our weaknesses as well as our strengths rather than to hide behind the neurotic mask of dishonesty. Such honesty should be tempered with love and consideration for others. Keith Miller discusses this in his second book.

I am NOT suggesting the starting of some sort of "honesty cult." Such groups are often harmful and almost invariably wind up being *un*Christian. The object . . . is not to reveal immoral and lascivious incidents. . . . One does not rip off his mask (or anyone else's). Rather he becomes willing for God to remove the unnecessary part of his facade gradually by providing the security he needs to be more honest. Also a ground rule in this type of group is never to share something in such a way that it may make *another* person vulnerable. The highest value in the Christian life is not honesty — but *love* (I Corinthians 13). This is a very important basic difference between Christian . . . and some . . . psychologically oriented groups.[18]

Rigidity

The lack of flexibility which is so characteristic of neurosis is also very common in the institutional church. Recently some members in a small-town church suggested that the morning offering be eliminated and that a "gift box" be placed in the back of the church. The reason for this suggestion was that most of the church members were hired by one big industry in the town. This company paid its employees monthly and the church members, most of whom tithed, placed their money in the plate at the first of the month and did not give again until the next month. A different manner of collecting tithes and offerings is a minor change but when it was suggested some of the church members became indignant. While the gift box idea was eventually put into practice (with no loss in monthly income) this situation illustrates some of the rigidity which is characteristic of many Christians. We develop specific "techniques of witnessing," unchangeable formats for the worship services, pat answers to moral questions, and a well-established evangelical jargon to be used in prayer meetings and at testimony times. We teach Sunday School classes by the lecture method but fail to realize that modern educational theory has demonstrated more effective ways of reaching young people. We continue to hold week-long evangelistic and missionary crusades but forget that committed Christians have a number of other responsibilities which make legitimate demands on their time during the week. We persist with the 11 A.M. worship hour — a practice which apparently began in rural churches many years ago to accommodate farmers who came to church after completing the morning chores — and never stop to consider that for some congregations another time might be more desirable.

Many of these traditions in the church, originally get their start at home. Under the guise of "good discipline", parents sometimes impose strict and rigid rules on their children, making demands that are almost impossible to meet. The child with limited ability who is expected to get high grades, or the active youngster who must always be a model of good behavior in church, eventually concludes that he "can't do it, so why try?" Such children often become insecure, anxious, and plagued with guilt feelings. Frequently they are hostile and rebellious but many times they develop rigid, restrictive personalities showing exaggerated conformity to rules or regulations coupled with an inability to tolerate non-conformity in others.

Christians who train their children in this rigid way are often making a sincere attempt to follow Biblical principles. Scripture teaches parents to train their children and this includes discipline.[19] But to make cold, rigid, perfectionistic demands which are beyond the child's capacity to obey is to train up a child who will be a legalistic, neurotic, and perhaps resentful Christian. Paul recognized that such discipline would adversely affect children. "Don't keep on scolding and nagging your children, making them angry and resentful," he wrote, "but bring them up with the love and discipline the Lord himself approves, with suggestions and godly advice.[20]

There is nothing wrong with tradition in the church

but we should not persist in outdated practices which are based on experience but treated as if they were Biblical truths. Jesus demonstrated his flexibility by the way in which He dealt with different people. With Nicodemus, Jesus carried on an intellectual discussion. With the Pharisees, He quoted scripture. With the money-changers in the temple He used what looks very much like physical violence, but with the sick lady who had "an issue of blood" He displayed extreme concern and gentleness. Paul showed similar flexibility while he was waiting for Silas and Timothy in Athens. With the Jews and religious leaders Paul argued in the synagogue, with others he held dialogue in the market-place, and with the philosophers and intellectuals the apostle gave a formal lecture on Mars Hill.[21]

The rigidity which tends to be characteristic of many local churches prevents us from bringing the gospel to lost men and women and opens us to the charge of irrelevancy. I would not agree with some modern theologians who are of the opinion that the answer to rigidity in the church is a change in doctrine. There is no Biblical justification for changing our doctrine to fit the desires of men. Instead, I must agree with the speaker at an Inter-Varsity missionary convention who suggested that God wants people who are conservative in theology and progressive in every other area.[22]

Difficult Interpersonal Relations

People who are insecure and trying to exert their superiority, people who are dishonest, and people who are rigid, are likely to have difficulty in getting along with each other. It is not surprising then, that at least some people in the church act in ways which prevent smooth interpersonal relations. Let us look at difficulties between people within the church and then look at conflicts between church members and the non-believers outside of the church.

Internal difficulties. Strife within the church is very old. In Acts, Chapter 15, the Jews and the Gentiles got into a big dispute over the extent to which the church members should participate in Jewish ceremonial. Each side believed that they were acting in accordance with the will of God and neither side was willing to give in to the other.

In more recent times the issues over which we argue are different, but men still rise up against men, all of whom honestly believe that their position is scripturally sound. Such factions forget that different parts of the body of Christ cannot remain strong if they are fighting against each other.[23] In criticizing church dissension, I do not advocate a wishy-washy Christianity. At times we must take a stand for our beliefs, but much of the dissension within the church today is over insignificant issues and can hardly be described as psychologically healthy.

There are other examples of poor relationships between believers. The pious Pharisee type who has such high expectations for others that he rarely stoops to get involved in the Lord's work; the detached personality, coldly disinterested in the church's activities; the parasite personality clinging to the pastor or to anyone else willing to show sympathy and interest are examples of church people who do not get along well with others in the congregation.

External Difficulties. Sometimes people within the church don't get along well with people outside of the church because they expect outsiders to conform to Christian standards. If a non-believer uses foul language or engages in behavior considered to be unchristian, we tend to reject him. Before long, justified by the belief that we are not to be of this world and

that we should not be unequally yoked with unbelievers, we withdraw into our own little Christian communities. Our friends are all Christians, our children attend
Christian schools, we listen to Christian radio stations,
and read Christian books. We patronize Christian
businessmen and go to Christian doctors regardless of
their medical competence. As a result of this inbreed-
ing we become "Protestant monks" unable to communicate with people in the world around us let alone
witness to them.

When Jesus prayed for the church, he did not ask
that we should be taken out of the world, but that we
should be kept from the world's evil.[24] The Christian
who withdraws into his own little group and is not
willing to interact with people in the market-place will
not have good relationships with non-believers.

Perhaps there is one other neurotic tendency displayed by some people within the church which makes
for strained relationships between church people and
those on the outside. This is what one writer has called
"religious kookishness".[25] While this may be rare, we
do put a strain on interpersonal relations when we
make sensational prophetic statements about events in
our world (especially when such statements are based
on tenuous scriptural evidence); criticize education (a
form of kookishness which thankfully is disappearing
from the church); become suspicious of medical treatment such as fluoridation, blood transfusions, or drugs;
and associate ourselves with all kinds of far out political causes. The tragedy of this kind of kooky behavior
is that it makes the gospel appear kooky also. Augus-
tine was concerned about the same problem in the
fifth century.

When they (unbelievers) find one belonging to the Christian body, falling into error on a subject with which they

themselves are thoroughly conversant, and when they see him, moreover, enforcing his groundless opinion by the authority of our sacred books, how are they likely to put trust in these books about the resurrection of the dead, and the hope of eternal life, and the kingdom of heaven.[26]

Scripture appears to give a number of guidelines concerning interpersonal behavior. If the love is in us which was also in Christ Jesus then we will show the same kind of love for other people that He showed. He did not always approve of the ways in which other people acted, but He did have such a concern for men that He was willing to die for them.[27] A love for one another within the church and for those outside of the church is something which is divinely given when our life is controlled by the Holy Spirit.[28] It is then that we can "fight the good fight of faith" and cease struggling with our fellow men.

Guilt

For a long time psychologists have been interested in guilt because they have recognized that this is the basis of much neurotic behavior. Guilt has been defined as "the realization that one has violated ethical or moral or religious principles, together with the regretful feeling of lessened personal worth" because of this.[29] It is a form of self-blame which is present to some degree and at some times in all of us. The boy who goes skiing and leaves the walk unshoveled, the Sunday School teacher who neglects to prepare his lesson, the driver who accelerates in order to get through a yellow light, the pastor who "puts off" making a call to some complaining shut-in — these are everyday examples of situations which can produce feelings of guilt.

There are broad individual differences in the extent to which one is bothered by guilt. Some people can

murder and apparently feel no guilt. Others feel guilty
about walking across a lawn and ignoring a "keep off
the grass" sign. It is likely that some guilt feelings are
unconscious while others are conscious. When guilt
feelings are so strong that they prey on an individual's
mind, they frequently form the basis of neurosis.

Psychologists and theologians have often disagreed
over the issue of guilt. Christians have pointed out that
if we do not experience a sense of guilt for our sinfulness, we can never come to know Christ. Some psychologists have emphasized that guilt feelings are bad
and should be overcome. Writing in a psychological
journal a few years ago, one psychologist stated that
"giving anyone a sense of . . . guilt or self-blame is the
worst possible way to help him to be an emotionally
sound and adequately socialized individual." This psychologist suggests that talk about sin and guilt is "the
direct and indirect cause of virtually all neurotic disturbance."[30]

One of the most helpful attempts to grapple with this
area of conflict between psychology and Christianity
has been presented by a Christian psychiatrist in a
book entitled *Guilt and Grace*.[31] The author suggests
that there are two kinds of guilt. "True guilt" is the
result of disobedience to God. It comes from dependence on anything or anyone other than God. The church
can and *should* stimulate this kind of guilt. When we
recognize and feel guilty about our disobedience to God,
then we can see the need of asking for forgiveness and
experience the change which occurs when Christ lifts
the load of guilt.

In contrast, "false guilt" is that which results from
the judgments and suggestions of men. When we make
other people feel guilty because of the way they dress,
because of something they have said, or because of
time that they have wasted, we are building up a man-

made guilt which is at the basis of many neurotic symptoms.

Such false guilt *should not* be encouraged by the church. But it is! People are made to feel guilty because they are not participating in committee meetings, are being poor stewards of money, are uninvolved or unfaithful in attending meetings, church socials or other events. There is nothing wrong with reminding people of their spiritual obligations but too often we make people feel guilty, not because they have disobeyed God, but because they have refused to participate in all of the church's activities.

There is another way in which the church encourages guilt feelings. We have developed a number of statements about the ideal Christian life. These statements reflect misconceptions about Christianity. They are not Biblical but are widely held and when Christians find that these statements do not describe their own experience they feel guilty and spiritually defeated. Some examples of these misconceptions are as follows:

—The Christian who lives a life of obedience to God will never experience problems.
—There is a set of spiritual rules which, if followed, will eliminate turmoil and discouragement in life.
—If we become a Christian the painful remnants of all our past sins will be removed.
—Becoming a Christian will automatically bring perpetual peace, unending joy, material wealth, physical health, and success in life
—The committed Christian never has doubts, never feels angry or discouraged, can never become mentally ill, never experiences sexual impulses, and has no further desire to sin.

Each of these statements may be true of some people, but for most of us this is not an accurate description of our Christian lives. The apostle Paul was a committed believer but these are not descriptions of his life. When we fail to measure up to man-made standards such as these, guilt and sometimes neurosis results.[32] When the church perpetuates such ideas, it is creating guilt feelings and encouraging neurosis within its membership.

Double-Mindedness

According to the book of James, the double-minded man is unstable in all his ways.[33] While the church rarely encourages this, individual church members sometimes try to live in accordance with a double standard. They attempt to serve God on Sunday but forget about this for the rest of the week. This double-mindedness permits the individual to deny his responsibility of following Christ on a full time basis. Psychology and scripture are in agreement that one cannot function efficiently when attempting to live in accordance with two conflicting standards.

Dealing with Neurosis

In Chapter 9, we will consider some of the ways in which mental disorders are treated. At this point let us risk oversimplification by suggesting three procedures which appear to be both psychologically and scripturally sound and which can help us deal with neurosis in the church.

1. *Recognize the problem.* One of the basic rules of clinical psychology is that we should be willing to face our problems and do something about them. This is also scriptural because the Bible teaches that men must face up to their sins and weaknesses. When a person recognizes his neurotic tendencies and acknowledges that they are present, he has made one of the biggest steps toward recovery.

2. *Confess our faults to God and to men.* "If we say

that we have no sin, we deceive ourselves, and the truth is not in us. If we confess our sins, he is faithful and just to forgive us our sins, and to cleanse us from all unrighteousness. .... Confess your faults one to another, and pray for one another."[34]

3. *Make an effort to change the situation.* None of these neurotic trends are based on scriptural teachings. All are based on traditions which might have served a worthwhile function in the past but which have become unhealthy in the church today. Such neurotic behavior can be changed but this will not be easy. A reconsideration of scriptural teachings concerning the church, the willing co-operation of sincere and honest Christians, and perhaps some professional guidance, may be necessary if we are to deal effectively with church neuroses. With the help of God, however, and with active involvement by church members, we can learn to be more flexible, more understanding, more loving, and less neurotic.

[1] *Acts 2:42; 4:31; 6:7; 4:32; 5:1-11.*

[2] *Acts 6:1; 15:2; Revelation 2:4, 10, 14, 20; 3:1, 17.*

[3] *Bishop John A. T. Robinson's* Honest to God *(Philadelphia: The Westminster Press, 1963) was a widely read criticism of the "conventional thought patterns of the church." Pierre Berton's* The Comfortable Pew *(Philadelphia: J. B. Lippincott, 1965) is an outsider's view of the church. Helmut Thielicke gives an insider's view in his book,* The Trouble With the Church: A Call for Renewal. *New York: Harper and Row, 1965. The Roman Catholic view is presented by a former priest, James Kavanaugh,* A Modern Priest Looks at His Outdated Church *(New York: Trident Press, 1967). A novel,* Holy Masquerade *(Grand Rapids, Michigan: Wm. B. Eerdmans, 1963) gives the view of a Swedish pastor, Olav Hartman, who is concerned about hypocrisy in the church.*

[4] *James A. Pike, Religion and Rebellion.* Psychology Today, *Vol. I, August 1967, p. 46. Copyright © Communications/Research/Machines/Inc. Quoted by permission.*

[5] *Robert James St. Clair,* Neurotics in the Church. *Westwood, New Jersey: Revell, 1963, p. 17.*

[6] *Samuel B. Kutash, Psychoneurosis. In Benjamin B. Wolman (editor),* Handbook of Clinical Psychology. *New York: McGraw-Hill, 1965, p. 949.*

[7] *See James C. Coleman,* Abnormal Psychology and Modern Life *(Third edition). Chicago: Scott, Foresman, 1964. A concise statement of neurotic characteristics appears on pages 193-195.*

[8] *J. F. Brown,* Psychodynamics of Abnormal Behavior. *New York: McGraw-Hill, 1940.*

[9] *Matthew 11:28-30.*

[10] *Romans 3:23.*

[11] *Isaiah 64:6; Romans 3:10.*

[12] *Romans 3:23-24; Living Letters phrases these verses as follows: "All have sinned; all fall short of God's glorious ideal; yet now God declares that we are good in His sight if we trust in Jesus Christ, Who freely takes away our sins." See also Romans 8:14.*

[13] *Eric Berne,* Games People Play: The Psychology of Human Relationships. *New York: Grove Press, 1964.*

[14] *Judi Culbertson and Patti Bard,* Games Christians Play. *New York: Harper and Row, 1967.*

[15] *James 2:2-9.*

[16] *Colossians 3:9-11; Galatians 3:28.*

[17] *Keith Miller,* The Taste of New Wine. *Waco, Texas: Word Books, 1965, pp. 22, 27. Quoted by permission.*

[18] *Keith Miller,* A Second Touch. *Waco, Texas: Word Books, 1967, p. 142. Quoted by permission.*

[19] *Proverbs 22:6, 13.*

[20] *Ephesians 6:4, Living Letters.*

[21] *Acts 17:16-32.*

[22] *Eric Fife, as reported in* Christianity Today, *Vol. 12, January 19, 1968, p. 36.*

[23] *I Corinthians 12:12-31.*

[24] *John 17:15-18.*

[25] *John W. Montgomery, Down with Kookishness,* Eternity, *Vol. 18, July 1967, p. 9ff.*

[26] *Quoted in Montgomery, Ibid. p. 35.*

[27] *Romans 5:8; I John 3:16.*

[28] *Galatians 5:22; I Thessalonians 3:12.*

[29] *H. B. English and Ava C. English,* A Comprehensive Dictionary of Psychological and Psychoanalytic Terms. *New York: Longmans, Green and Co., 1958. p. 234.*

[30] *A. Ellis, "There is No Place for the Concept of Sin in Psychotherapy."* Journal of Consulting Psychology. *1960, 7.*

[31] *Paul Tournier,* Guilt and Grace, *New York: Harper and Row, 1958.*

[32] *Some of the ideas in this section were taken from a book by Marion H. Nelson,* Why Christians Crack Up, *Chicago, Illinois: Moody Press, 1960.*

[33] *James 1:8.*

[34] *I John 1:8, 9; James 5:16.*

8

NEUROSIS IN SOCIETY

The church is not the only organization which stimulates the anxiety, rigidity, inefficiency, discouragement, and unhappiness of neurosis. Our whole Western culture exhibits and encourages behavior, which, in the opinion of some psychologists, is "sick".

Much has been written about the unhealthy social tendencies which are assumed to characterize our sick society. For the most part, however, this chapter will be limited to a consideration of neurotic trends that have been discussed by some better known psychologists. Once again, each of the issues will be considered in the light of Biblical revelation.

Anxiety

The word "anxiety" refers to an emotional experience which most people feel at one time or another but which few are able to define accurately. Although psychological definitions differ, for our purposes we can think of anxiety as an emotional state characterized by apprehension, uneasiness, and fear.

It is possible to identify two types of anxiety. Specific anxiety results when we are aware of some recognizable threatening object or situation. The church member who gets up to present a report at the business meeting, the student who is in the classroom waiting for the teacher to hand out an examination paper or the person who almost loses his balance on a slippery sidewalk, all experience a period of anxiety because they are afraid of what might happen if they give a poor speech, fail the test, or fall on the ice. Free-floating anxiety is an emotional reaction which occurs in the absence of obvious threat. The person who experiences free-floating anxiety is afraid that "something terrible is going to happen", but he does not know what it is. Although this anxiety is not common in the general population, it is frequently seen in psychiatric patients. Probably most of our anxiety is somewhere between the specific and the free-floating. The mother who worries while her child is at camp or the father who is apprehensive when his teen-age son first uses the family car are each experiencing an anxiety which is partially specific and partially free-floating. Each feels a vague (free-floating) uneasiness centering around a number of possible (specific) mishaps that might occur.

Within recent years psychologists have stressed the extent to which anxiety has crept into our society. Anxiety has been called "the official emotion of our age," the most pervasive psychological phenomenon of our time, and the emotion of "central significance" in all abnormal behavior. Others have suggested that we are living in an age of anxiety.[1]

What causes anxiety? Psychologists do not know for sure but a number of plausible explanations have been suggested. One writer, for example, has suggested that "the causes of contemporary anxiety are complex: two world wars within our century, and the cold war persisting since the last one; enormous mobility of peoples, geographically and economically, disturbing the sense of rootedness; shifting values, so that we are uncertain about child-rearing practices, about moral standards, about religious beliefs."[2] Freud believed that anxiety arose from three sources: threats in the external world, a concern lest our secret desires and impulses somehow get out and take control of our behavior, or a fear that our conscience might bring about intense feelings of guilt or shame.[3] Some experimental psychologists have suggested that we learn to be anxious while we are growing up and facing conflicts. Finally, Dr. Hobart Mowrer of the University of Illinois has concluded that anxiety results from guilt over some act which we have committed, but wish that we had not done.[4]

All of these are plausible explanations and most of them have been supported by experimental research or by the careful observation of anxious people. Two other causes of anxiety might be added to this list, however: fear of failure and technological change.

Recently I invited some of my students to list the things which they most feared. Of about one hundred students who responded to my question, over half indicated that their greatest fear was failure. Our Western culture has placed great emphasis on succeeding and getting ahead. We reward success with approval, status, and money. Early in life our children are taught the importance of successful accomplishments. Our schools and colleges have become centers of intensive competition which carries over into the business and professional world and often creeps into the church. Of course, the maintenance of high standards and the desire for success is not bad in itself. Undoubtedly the struggle to get ahead has lead to much of our social progress and technological advance. Everybody is not going to succeed in reaching his high goals, however. This realization, coupled with a fear of failure, is undoubtedly the cause of much contemporary anxiety.

Then there is technological change! If all of the world's scientists throughout the ages of history were brought back to life, they would be greatly outnumbered by the scientists who are living and working in our day. Scientific knowledge has produced rapid technical change which is unmatched by any other period in history. With the benefits of technological development, there has also come greater stress, increased anxiety, and a rise in the prevalence of neurosis.

In considering how change can create anxiety and neurosis, let us look at the matter of values. As technology has advanced, traditional values, loyalties, and ideals seem to have become outdated. Former values no longer appear able to give clear direction to the individual who must cope with this changing world and make decisions concerning his uncertain future. Living in a society where old ideas are constantly replaced with new ways of doing things, it is hardly surprising that people throw over old values and attempt to replace them with something new. As a result many individuals are "groping about, bewildered and bitter, unable to find ... values which will enable them to live satisfying, fulfilling, and meaningful lives."[5] Thus with all of its benefits, technological change can also bring confusion over values, with a resulting increase in anxiety and insecurity.

Biblical Views of Anxiety

In older translations of the Bible the word "fear" is used often to mean something similar to what we call anxiety. Modern versions are more likely to use the term "anxiety." In either case, the cause and the cure of this condition appear to be the same. Men become anxious because they forget about Christ. Anxiety is reduced (although perhaps not eliminated) by an increased dependence on Christ.

Consider, for example, the words of Jesus when He was preaching the Sermon on the Mount. "Do not be anxious about your life, what you shall eat or what you shall drink, nor about your body, what you shall put on." If we believe God supplies men's needs we need not worry.[6] Paul gives similar advice in his letter to the Philippians. "Have no anxiety about anything, but in everything by prayer and supplication with thanksgiving let your requests be made known unto God. And the peace of God which passes all understanding, will keep your hearts and your minds in Christ Jesus."[7] Peter gave us the same message when he wrote, "Cast all your anxieties on Him, for He cares about you."[8] A number of Old Testament writers say much the same thing.[9]

Before leaving our discussion on anxiety, it might be well to point out that in small doses anxiety is not abnormal, unhealthy, or even bad. Some anxiety is a part of life which adds excitement and motivates us in times when we do not feel enthusiastic. Most of us would probably never have gone far in school had we not experienced some anxiety prior to the taking of tests. Such a mild anxiety is a part of life for which we can be thankful. But scripture verses dealing with this topic make no distinction between extreme and mild anxiety. Clearly there is a divine source of help for handling all anxiety regardless of its intensity.

Meaninglessness

While some people are convinced that anxiety is the major source of neurosis in our society, there are others who feel that the chief problem of people in the twentieth century is emptiness, a lack of purpose in life, or a lack of meaning.

Undoubtedly the best-known spokesman for this view is Dr. Victor E. Frankl. In chapter five we briefly mentioned Frankl's experiences in a Nazi prison camp during the Second World War. Recently Frankl was interviewed in a national magazine and expressed his current views about the lack of meaning in people's lives:

More and more patients are approaching psychiatrists with the complaint of an inner void and emptiness, with a sense of meaninglessness, with a feeling of a total and ultimate futility of life.... Unlike an animal man is not told by his instincts what he must do. And, in contrast to man in former days, he doesn't even know what he basically wishes to do. And what is the result? Either he simply does what other people do or ... another effect is neuroticism — a ... despair over the apparent meaninglessness of life.[10]

The beatnik movement of the early 1960s and the hippie philosophy of the mid-sixties are monuments to the lack of meaning and purpose in many lives. Numerous young people have rebelled against the values and goals of an older generation. They do not like established society because they recognize that much adult behavior is phony. As a result, some young people have thrown over long-established values, and because they have nothing with which to replace these values, they live only for the experience of the present. If LSD or Yogi or some other technique gives an apparent meaning to life here and now, it is easy to ignore the long-range consequences of behavior.

The Bible makes a number of statements about values and about man's purpose for existing. Biblical writers viewed life as something which was very temporary. James referred to life as a vapour or puff of smoke, and the Psalmist called life an evening shadow.[11] We must live, therefore, with the recognition that God's will can overshadow all our plans and expectations.

This does not mean, however, that we should live, eat, and be merry now since tomorrow we might die. God sent His Son not only to make possible an eternal life in the future but to give an abundant life in the present. The eternal life comes through belief in Christ, and the abundant life comes from the acceptance of a number of values which are described in the Bible. For example, real purpose and meaning in the present life comes from following Jesus Christ and becoming His disciple rather than seeking status or accumulating earthly treasures. Biblical values would have us "work at what is right and good, learning to trust Him and love others, and to be patient and gentle."[12]

Discouragement

Every year in the United States an estimated 200,000 people attempt suicide. Of these, several thousand are successful and it may be that many more deaths which are attributed to natural or accidental causes really result from suicide. Most of the people who attempt to take their own lives are discouraged or despondent. Clearly this is a major unhealthy trend in twentieth century society.

Psychological studies have shown that the majority of persons who attempt suicide make their intention known or give some clues in advance. A number of suicide prevention centers have been established to counsel with people who are contemplating suicide and to provide information about the causes of self-destruction. Because of these centers, the number of suicides has been decreasing.[13]

But how does one prevent or treat the depression and discouragement which sometimes becomes so intense that it causes an individual to consider suicide? Why do all of us become at least mildly depressed at times? Before attempting to answer these different questions we should look at the characteristics of the person who is discouraged.

In addition to despondency, despair, and a generally bleak outlook on life, the depressed individual often shows three kinds of behavior. First there is complaining and criticism. Sometimes discouraged people criticize those with whom they live; they criticize their employers; they may criticize God; and very frequently they are critical of themselves. Secondly, we notice self-pity. One psychiatrist has described this as the "poor little me" outlook on life. Thirdly there is an inertia and unwillingness to be active. Since life is so unhappy there hardly seems any purpose in doing much of anything. As a result the individual does nothing and in extreme cases decides to end his misery by death.

As with most human behavior the causes of discouragement are varied. Usually some stress enters our lives which we are unable to overcome or rise above. Perhaps we blame ourselves or someone else for the difficulty, and we react with feelings of hopelessness.

The Bible contains many scenes of discouragement. When Moses was leading the children of Israel through the desert he reached a period of depression in which he expressed a wish to die. When Joshua took over leadership of the people he also experienced periods of discouragement. Job was discouraged in the midst of his tribulations, and the prophet Jeremiah showed the same reaction.[14] In the New Testament, Jesus witnessed a great scene of discouragement when He arrived in Bethany following the death of Lazarus. Mary and Martha were grieving, Thomas had lost hope, and the Jews were critical.[15] In Luke 24 we see that the followers of Jesus were sad[16] and in Romans 7 there is evidence to suggest that the Apostle Paul had periods of despondency.[17] Perhaps one of the most interesting examples of discouragement is recorded in the twenty-first chapter of Numbers. In their wilderness journey the children of Israel requested permission to take a short cut through the land of Edom. When the Edomites refused this request and the Israelites discovered that they would have to travel many extra miles to go around Edom, the people became very discouraged. They began to complain and be critical. They felt sorry for themselves and decided that they were probably going to die in the wilderness.[18]

When a person is discouraged it is often difficult to help him overcome his feelings. The Israelites needed to be jolted out of their despondency and apparently this is what God did. In any case, the treatment which got the Israelites moving again might also be effective with depressed people today. The children of Israel did two things. First, they made use of their spiritual resources. Apparently they had forgotten about God — except to criticize — but when they confessed their sins, returned again to prayer and put their trust in the power of God, things improved. Secondly, they took practical steps to overcome the problem. Perhaps they didn't feel like pressing on with their long journey but they must have realized that sitting and complaining in the wilderness was not going to do them any good. So they moved on!

In the twentieth century we might take a lesson from these Israelites. But it remains difficult to motivate people who are depressed. Modern medicine has developed a number of effective anti-depressant drugs but these are only temporary relief measures. As long as our society is complicated, anxiety prone, and characterized by little direction or meaning, it will continue to be a society which is also characterized by despondency and discouragement. Once again it would appear that the indwelling power of the Holy Spirit is the only really effective and permanent answer to the problem of discouragement.

Conformity

Several years ago Erich Fromm wrote a book in which he suggested that as man has developed through history he has become isolated and lonely. But man does not like to feel independent. Indeed, Fromm suggested, man wants to experience a sense of belonging and a feeling of rootedness.

Perhaps in his attempt to belong, modern man has been seized with the need to conform. One psychologist has indicated that we do not like to consider ourselves conformists, so instead of telling people to "conform" we tell them to "adjust". Indeed, says Dr. Robert Lindner, the theme of modern behavior is "the eleventh commandment . . . You Must Adjust!" This "commandment" dominates the nursery where we shape children to conform to society; it is the guiding philosophy in our public education; it is the slogan of all political parties;it is "the command etched above the door of every church, synagogue, cathedral, temple, and chapel;" and it is the psychologist's answer for anxiety and personal problems.[20] Even the youthful rebel, who makes so much of his independence and non-conformity, behaves in ways which are similar to other so-called non-conformists.

To see conformity listed as a neurotic trend may

come as a surprise to some readers. Normally we consider conformity to be good and assume that the non-conformist is odd and dissatisfied. Is it possible that the extreme conformity about which Lindner writes and the apparent non-conformity of beatniks and hippies are equally unhealthy and unscriptural? When man conforms like a robot, life will be unhappy and discouraging. Likewise, when man shows a lack of conformity and becomes a social rebel, he is anxious and unhappy.

More to be desired is a position between the extremes of over-conformity and non-conformity. Noah, Abraham, Joseph, Moses, Jesus, Peter, and all the other great men of the Bible conformed to the will of God but they did not adjust well to the expectations of the societies in which they lived. Modern man whose life is guided by scripture must also expect to be somewhat of a social non-conformist whose mind has been transformed by the Holy Spirit to conform to the perfect will of God.[21]

Busyness

Why are people so busy today? Why the frenzied activity and the hectic pace which seems to characterize all levels of our society? In past years, this busyness with its resulting tension and insecurity was thought to be the distinctive mark of businessmen. Today, however, busy activity has become typical of almost everybody. Because we recognize the importance of stimulation for young children, we keep our youngsters involved in all kinds of activities. By the time they get into high school they are sometimes the busiest people in the family with schoolwork, extra-curricular activities, dating, church events, part-time jobs, music lessons, sports, and numerous other time-consuming interests. Modern college students, for the most part, have little time for the parties and enthusiastic school spirit of past decades. The pressures of academic requirements and the need for so many of them to work at part-time jobs keeps them "on the go" seven days a week. Housewives, professional men, businessmen — all are busy. The invention of labor-saving and time-saving devices should have given us more leisure time, but we have filled this increased "free" time with additional frenzied activity. Even the church has become the center of numerous meetings and activities which sometimes keep the faithful occupied every night of the week.

While psychologists have been interested in the causes of this busyness, little has been written and almost no research done on the problem. All of us have had the experience of engaging in some kind of activity to distract ourselves from an unpleasant or threatening situation. It is common knowledge that grief-stricken people often get busy so they can, at least temporarily, forget their loss. Might it be that some of our busyness is an attempt to distract ourselves from the anxiety, meaninglessness, discouragement, and overconformity of modern life? If we are busy there is less need to face the anxiety that comes with fear of failure or technological change. Perhaps if we keep involved in numerous activities (especially when they are worthwhile activities), we will not have to face the frustrations, lack of values, and futility in our lives. If we keep busy, we can ignore the fact that we are all conformists whose very busyness is an act of conformity.

It is possible that activity gives us an excuse to avoid responsibility. Obviously there are many busy people whose numerous activities are worthwhile and who competently shoulder many important responsibilities. Nevertheless, for others, "I'm too busy" really means

"I'm too lazy", "I don't want to be involved" or "I don't want to take on responsibility."

There is nothing wrong with being busy. Physiological psychologists tell us that our brain and mental capacities are only used to a portion of their potential. If we can accomplish things, it is surely wrong to waste time doing nothing. Nevertheless, we must remember that even the busiest men mentioned in scripture periodically slowed down. In the course of His ministry Jesus was probably one of the most active men in His part of the world but He regularly took time for prayer. This coming apart to "be still" in the presence of God not only renewed Christ spiritually, but seems to have been His way of slowing down. It was recommended by the Psalmist[22] and may be the scriptural answer for busyness and for other neurotic trends in our society.

Conclusion

Neurotic behavior is not confined to Christians, nor is neurosis stimulated solely by the church. We live in a society and period of history which encourage neurosis and stimulate anxiety, meaninglessness, discouragement, conformity, and busyness in people of all faiths.

Can anything be done to eliminate or at least reduce the neurotic behavior within the church and without? The Word of God makes some statements about men's needs and frustrations, but so does modern psychology. It might be asked if this relatively new science is effective or even necessary for treating neurosis and other forms of abnormal behavior. These issues are discussed in the next chapter.

[1] *Quoted in Eugene E. Levitt,* The Psychology of Anxiety, *Indianapolis: Bobbs-Merrill, 1967, pp. vii, 1; copyright © 1967. Reprinted by permission.*

[2] *Ernest R. Hilgard,* Ibid., *p. vii.*

[3] Ibid., *p. 22.*

[4] *O. Hobart Mowrer,* The Crisis in Psychiatry and Religion. *Princeton, New Jersey: Van Nostrand, 1961, p. 68.*

[5] *James C. Coleman,* Abnormal Psychology and Modern Life. *(Third edition.) Chicago: Scott-Foresman, 1964, p. 160.*

[6] *Matthew 6:25, 31, 34; Revised Standard Version.*

[7] *Philippians 4:6-7; Revised Standard Version.*

[8] *I Peter 5:7; Revised Standard Version.*

[9] *Genesis 26:24; Numbers 14:9; Psalm 23:4, 56:4, 118:6; Isaiah 41:10; 43:5.*

[10] *Mary Harrington Hall, A Conversation with Viktor Frankl of Vienna.* Psychology Today, *February 1958, Vol. 1, pp. 56-63. Copyright © Communications/Research/Machines/Inc. Quoted by permission.*

[11] *James 4:14; Psalm 102:11.*

[12] *The arguments in this part in the chapter are supported by the following Bible verses: John 3:16; 6:40-47; 10:10 Matthew 16:19-20, 24-27; Luke 9:23-26; and I Timothy 6:7-10. The quotation is from I Timothy 6:11, Living Letters.*

[13] *The telephone numbers of suicide prevention centers are usually listed in the telephone book. Mental health associations can also provide information concerning local counseling facilities.*

[14] *Numbers 11:15; Joshua 7:7; Job 10:1; Jeremiah 15:10.*

[15] *John 11:19, 16, 37.*

[16] *Luke 24:17b.*

[17] *See especially verses 18-25.*

[18] *Numbers 20:21; 21:4-5.*

[19] *Numbers 21:6.*

[20] *Robert Lindner,* Must You Conform? *New York: Holt, Rinehart and Winston, 1956, pp. 167, 170.*

[21] *Romans 12:1-2.*

[22] *Psalm 46:10.*

9

TREATMENT OF EMOTIONAL DISORDERS

What is the difference between a psychologist and a psychiatrist? This is probably the question which is most often asked when people meet psychologists in non-professional situations. Since this is a book on psychology, the preceding chapters have only mentioned psychiatry in one or two places. Before discussing treatment techniques we should distinguish between the mental health professions. While these professions have some activities — such as interviewing — which are common to all, each group is trained to bring a special contribution to the treatment program.

The *clinical psychologist* attends college for four years, followed by an additional four or five years of graduate school and completes at least a year of practical experience as a psychological intern. At the end of this training he receives a Ph.D. in clinical psychology. In most states and several Canadian provinces he then takes examinations to be certified as a psychologist. Upon completion of this training he is qualified to conduct interviews and to treat individuals or groups of people who have problems. The psychologist's most unique contribution comes in the areas of testing and research. The clinical psychologist is highly skilled in the designing, administration and interpretation of psychological tests. This training also gives him a special knowledge of scientific methods and because of this the psychologist is often involved in conducting research regarding the causes and treatment of mental illness.

It should not be assumed that all psychologists are clinical psychologists. Less than half of the psychologists in North America work with disturbed people. The remainder are involved in teaching, research, personnel work, industrial consultation, or a host of other activities. Sometimes a *non*-clinical psychologist, by his own admission, knows little more about abnormal behavior and its treatment than does the man on the street.

The *psychiatrist* is a medical doctor. Like all physicians, he must complete four years of college and four years of medical school, before he receives the M.D. degree. He then takes a year of internship followed by a three or four year psychiatric residency. This involves classroom work, study, and supervised contact with psychiatric patients. At the completion of this training he takes examinations which test his competence to be a psychiatrist. In working with the emotionally disturbed, the psychiatrist is concerned with the diagnosis and treatment of abnormality. Because of his medical training, he is qualified to prescribe drugs, conduct physical examinations, and use medical techniques of treatment. Psychiatrists are usually interested in research, but because of the nature of their training and the demands for their skills, few are actively engaged in scientific research.

The *psychiatric social worker* also takes four years of undergraduate college work, often with a pre-social work major. This is followed by two years of graduate study which leads to a master of social work degree. A few psychiatric social workers have doctorates. Like the other professionals, the social worker is involved in group and individual counseling, but probably his greatest contribution is to serve as a link between the patient and his family. The social worker interviews families in order to get background information, helps the family to understand something about the patient's problems, helps the patient to "fit in" when he returns home following treatment, and sometimes conducts group interviews with the whole family. Table 8-1 summarizes the differences between the three major mental health professions.

The *psychoanalyst* is a psychiatrist with several years of additional training in the specific treatment techniques and theories of Sigmund Freud and his followers. Psychoanalysis is the name given to the method which is used by psychoanalysts. Only a few psychiatrists have taken the long and specialized training which qualifies them to be psychoanalysts. Since their method of treatment is time consuming and expensive, they accept only a few people for treatment.

The *psychiatric nurse* is a registered nurse who has taken special additional training in psychology and psychiatry. She specializes in the nursing care of mental patients.

Common Treatment Techniques

If a person develops a psychological problem for which he needs help, what will the treatment be like? It is difficult to give a simple answer to this question because many different treatment techniques are currently in use and new procedures are always being developed. The treatment usually depends on the nature of the patient's disturbance, and on the personality, training, and theoretical position of the person (usually called the "therapist") who is giving the treatment.

TABLE 8-1.
THE MAJOR MENTAL HEALTH PROFESSIONS

Clinical Psychologist	Psychiatrist	Psychiatric Social Worker
Usual Training		
4 Years Undergraduate	4 Years Undergraduate	4 Years Undergraduate
4-5 Years Graduate School	4 Years Medical School	2 Years Graduate School
1-3 Years Psychological Internship and/or Post-doctoral training	1 Year Medical Internship 3-4 Years Psychiatric Residency	
Degree		
Ph.D.	**M.D.**	**M.S.W.**
Common Duties		
• Interviews	• Interviews	• Interviews
• Individual and Group Psychotherapy	• Individual and Group Psychotherapy	• Individual and Group Psychotherapy
• Psychological Testing	• Medical Treatment	• Working with the family and community
• Research	• Some research	

In spite of this variety of techniques, it is possible to identify a few procedures which are widely used by professionals in the mental health field.

Medical Treatment Techniques

The psychiatrist or other medically trained therapist may use any of the procedures which are common in modern medicine. Since many psychological problems are the direct result of physical illnesses, it is not surprising that surgery, a change in diet or a program of physical exercise might be effective. Shock therapy is another medical technique which in some way alleviates the symptoms of people who are depressed.

At present, however, the administration of drugs is the most widely used medical procedure. Some drugs, known as *tranquillizers,* are able to reduce an individual's anxiety and calm him down so that he feels less tense and more relaxed. Other drugs, usually called *anti-depressants,* stimulate depressed people so that they feel less discouraged and more willing to meet the challenges of life. The invention of drugs such as these has revolutionized the field of psychiatry, but it must be remembered that drugs are not "cure-alls". Problems which are caused by stress, failure, guilt feelings, or family turmoil, for example, can hardly be eliminated with drugs. Nevertheless, such medication helps the individual to feel better and makes him more able to grapple with his problems under the guidance of a professional counselor.

Non-medical Treatment Techniques

When an individual is troubled about some problem, he will often talk to a friend or seek the advice of a professional counselor. *Psychotherapy* is a form of treatment in which a troubled individual and a skilled counselor talk together. There are a number of different ways in which the counseling session might be conducted. The therapist may simply listen to the patient's problem and serve as a "sympathetic ear", or he may be more involved by giving reassurance, encouragement, suggestions, or advice. The process may be brief, lasting for one or two sessions, or it may continue for several years. The therapist may work with one person at a time or he may work with several people in a group. Since this is not the place to go into a detailed discussion of the different approaches which a therapist might use, we will limit ourselves to a brief description of some of the more common psychotherapy techniques.[1]

Psychoanalysis is a form of treatment based on the teachings of Freud. The patient lies on a couch and talks about whatever comes to his mind. The therapist seeks to understand the meaning of this talk, and attempts to assist the patient in gaining insight into his behavior. This is an expensive treatment technique which usually continues for several years.

Client-centered therapy (also known as non-directive therapy) assumes that man is quite capable of solving his own problems. The therapist tries to be an accepting friend who listens to the individual and helps him to get a better perspective on life. The person with the problem is called the client and the therapy is "client-centered" because improvement depends on the client's ability to work out solutions to his own difficulties.

Learning therapy is a relatively new treatment technique which is based on the assumption that all behavior — including problem behavior — is learned. The therapist, then, becomes a teacher who might use a number of learning techniques to get rid of the problem and to teach the individual how to act in a more desirable fashion.

Logotherapy is a procedure that Frankl has developed. The patient is presumed to lack purpose in life, and the goal of treatment is to find meaning. There is no attempt to force the therapist's views on the patient. Instead, it is assumed that the meaning of life differs from person to person and that somehow each patient will be able to "find" his own meaning.

Group therapy is a type of treatment in which a therapist meets with a group of people. The group members discuss their own problems and feelings with each other while the therapist encourages conversation, keeps the topic from wandering too far from its original point, and sometimes makes suggestions. Frequently, the group member is helped by realizing that others have problems similar to his. Often the group gives emotional support to an individual, and helps him to learn what behavior is acceptable to others. There is real value in seeing ourselves as others see us and the group provides this experience. In a sense, then, every group member is a therapist for every other.

While there have been a number of new developments in psychological treatment during the past few years, the growth of the group therapy movement has probably been the most significant. Of course this technique is not limited to mental patients. Groups of business executives, college students, housewives, professional people, and even neighbors regularly meet — often without a therapist — to discuss their mutual problems, anxieties, and discouragements. Family therapy is a special type of group therapy in which the members of a family get together to discuss their difficulties. It is not surprising that this recent upsurge in group discussion has attracted the attention of people within the church.

The Bible and Treatment Techniques

The Bible gives many illustrations of the ways in which problems were handled in the past.[2] Probably one of the earliest Biblical examples of counseling is reported in the book of Exodus.[3] Moses was spending his days listening to complaints, making legal judgments, and counseling with the people. The father-in-law of Moses, a man named Jethro, became concerned when he discovered that these counseling activities occupied Moses from morning to night. Jethro was afraid that the strain would be too much for his son-in-law and suggested that something should be done to share the work. It was probably with enthusiasm that Moses accepted this advice and chose a group of men to help with the governing and counseling. It is interesting to note that these were able, God-fearing, truthful, honest men, who were always available and who recognized the importance of referring difficult cases to someone who was more experienced.[4] As one writer has pointed out, even in this primitive setting we see some modern characteristics of effective counseling: organization, emphasis on moral qualifications, availability, and a system for referring difficult cases.

In another part of the Old Testament, we read of Job's tribulations and of the people who came to counsel with him. His wife recommended suicide. His friends, after a period of silence, tried to reason about the causes of the problem. When their intellectual interpretations were rejected they revealed their inability to be good counselors by turning against Job.

David, who gave so much comforting advice and counsel in the Psalms, was both familiar with the symptoms of abnormal behavior and effective as a counselor. One time when he was in danger he pretended to be mad and apparently was quite convincing.[5]

It is well known that David skillfully helped King Saul during his periods of emotional distress.[6]

When the birth of Jesus was foretold, the prophet said that "His name shall be called ... Counselor".[7] Many times we see that Jesus displayed the characteristics of a good counselor. He understood men.[8] He listened to them and He accepted them. Many of His statements were words of comfort, guidance, and encouragement. This concern for people was characteristic of Paul and others in the early church. We have already mentioned that men in the New Testament cast out demons — a technique which surely must be considered as a type of treatment for distraught individuals.

It is clear, therefore, that the Bible contains many examples of counseling. It also discusses ways in which men can deal with their personal problems and frustrations. Words of comfort, encouragement, guidance and help, are all found in the pages of scripture. But can we assume that a reading and acceptance of the Bible provides all of the answers to all of man's problems? This is a very important question. If we answer "no", we might be in danger of limiting the power of the Word of God. If we answer "yes", then Christians should have no need of psychologists, psychiatrists or other skilled counselors.

In dealing with this issue we might first look at the field of medicine. The God who gave man dominion over the earth,[9] has permitted medical science to gain considerable control over disease. Of course, the most significant medical advances have been made since the days when the New Testament was written. Thus, we do not expect scripture to mention modern medical techniques. Although it says much about the causes and treatment of disease, the Bible is not meant to be a technical medical textbook. This does not limit the

Words of God, nor does it eliminate physicians. They are applying skills that God in His sovereignty is permitting men to discover. As Christians, we can believe the scriptures and still patronize modern doctors.[10]

Similar conclusions apply in the treatment of psychological abnormalities. God, in His wisdom, has permitted psychologists and psychiatrists to develop modern treatment techniques which are not described in scripture. Although it contains many comforting words and says much about the causes and treatment of personal problems, the Bible is not a psychiatric textbook. This does not limit the Word of God — since it does not claim to provide specific answers to all of our problems — but neither does it eliminate psychologists and psychiatrists. If we are to deal successfully with abnormal behavior, a belief in the promises of Scripture and a reliance on the Lordship of Christ, must sometimes be coupled with the insights and methods of modern psychology. For this reason, the neurotic can benefit from the guidance and encouragement of a helpful pastor, a sympathetic friend, or a competent professional counselor.

Treatment Goals

In considering the goals of treatment we should remember the threefold definition of abnormality which was presented in chapter five. The individual can be considered abnormal, and thus in need of treatment, if he is at odds with the social expectations of his society, at odds with himself, and/or alienated from God.

When professional counselors work with disturbed individuals, their *stated* goals often differ. The counselor may attempt to change the counselee's view of the world and of himself, to teach him new ways of behaving, to create insight into the nature of his problem, to encourage him, to give practical suggestions, or to provide a situation where he can "let off steam". Most therapists hope that the counselee (sometimes called a client or patient) will learn to act in ways which are more consistent with the expectations of society and that his internal conflicts will be resolved or at least reduced. In helping people face their social problems and internal conflicts, the non-Christian therapist can often be effective in counseling with both non-believers and Christians. The counselee's relationship with God, however, is usually ignored. The professional counselor is not a missionary and in most cases has had no training in dealing with spiritual matters.

In contrast, the pastor's special area of competence concerns the individual's relationship with God. While the counselee's social behavior and internal conflicts may also be of concern, few ministers are trained to deal with these issues especially when they become complicated and lead to severe psychological disturbances. It is likely therefore, that the pastor will have goals that differ from those of the non-Christian therapist.

For several years psychologists and pastors have debated whether all of the counseling functions should or could be handled by one individual. Can a person, trained in both psychology and theology, assist disturbed individuals in their relationships with each other, with themselves, and with God? Some contemporary trends in both psychology and pastoral counseling have suggested that this *is* possible.

Recent Treatment Developments

Within recent years, an increasing number of Christians have been completing professional training and entering the mental health fields. Sometimes, these professional people take a year or two at seminary in order to sharpen their knowledge and appreciation of theological, Biblical and spiritual issues. When they enter their fields of service, these people are skilled in the use of psychological techniques and capable as spiritual counselors.

The number of competent Christian therapists, while increasing, is still small. But there are other indications that psychology and theology are beginning to work together in treating the emotionally disturbed. Among the most prominent of these indications are the most recent emphasis on values in psychology, the writings of O. Hobart Mowrer, and the expansion of the pastoral psychology movement.

Values

For many years young psychologists were taught that they should be completely neutral in counseling sessions. The therapist was warned that he should not try to impose his values on the patient. Instead, therapists were encouraged to become aware of their own value systems so that they could deliberately avoid indoctrinating their counselees. This view was based on the assumption that man is good, self-sufficient, and able to control his own destiny. Thus it was assumed that no counselor had any right — or need — to interfere with another man's value system.

Such a view placed psychologists and Christian counselors at odds with each other. The Christian believed that man was basically evil and unable to arrive at an acceptable value system. Many religious counselors felt that it was necessary to point out man's sinfulness so that he would recognize his alienation from God and hopefully come to a better understanding of his internal difficulties and strained relationships with other people.

This conflict was pointed out to men in a particularly dramatic way when I was employed in the counseling

center of a state university. One day a student came
into my office, flopped into a chair, and announced,
"My problem is that I don't have any values." As a
psychologist I was supposed to be neutral while helping
this young lady to find values. As a Christian I wanted
to be more directive in helping with her problem.
Rather than trying to remain neutral, I shared with
this student the value system which was meaningful
to me as a Christian. I did not force this on her and in
my opinion I was not "pushing religion." Instead I was
overtly sharing a part of the value system which gives
purpose to my life and guides all of my behavior, including my counseling.

Within recent years psychologists have come to realize that it is not possible to maintain complete neutral-
ity in counseling sessions. In a talk which she presented
a few years ago one of my former professors suggested
that "if a person interacts in any way with another
person, he is going to disseminate values. So he might
as well be explicit about it, admit it, and think about
it."[11] In psychological experiments conducted at Indi-
ana University, it was found that a counselor could
manipulate the behavior of a counselee by a simple
head nod or a few "uh-huh" responses. Even when he
tries to be neutral, therefore, a counselor's casual move-
ments and facial expressions subtly communicate his
own value system.

This realization has presented psychology with a
dilemma. Science, by definition, must be neutral but
psychologists now find that their beliefs are slipping
into their counseling sessions, sometimes unconsciously.
As a result, it is now being suggested that counselors
should recognize their own beliefs, confess that they
have biases, and attempt to be tolerant of other people's
values. Some writers are even suggesting that a psy-

chologist may be of greatest assistance to those people who share his beliefs.[12]

Clinical psychology and Christianity have discovered that they both have an interest in moral behavior and human values. Psychologists now show a greater tolerance for those who share values in counseling sessions. Of course, the therapist is not trained to be a religious counselor and is likely to be less explicit about values than is the pastor. But at least in this one area we now have more understanding and mutual respect between psychologists and pastoral counselors.

The Integrity Therapy of O. Hobart Mowrer

In the early years of his professional career, Dr. O. Hobart Mowrer distinguished himself as a research psychologist whose special interest was in the field of learning. His work was so widely recognized that in 1953 Mowrer was elected president of the American Psychological Association. On the day set for his installation into that office, however, the new president was absent. During his lifetime he had suffered from a series of emotional depressions and when he was due to take over the presidential duties he was a patient in a Chicago mental hospital.[13] Following his recovery, Mowrer concluded that instead of continuing as a researcher in experimental psychology he would devote the remainder of his life to a study of the causes and treatment of abnormal behavior. He began, to the surprise of his colleagues, by turning to the church to see if religion could meet man's needs. Mowrer is not a regular member of any church. He does not believe in a theistic God, and there is little likelihood that he accepts the Bible as the divine Word of God. In spite of this he has made some interesting observations which have paved the way for a greater rapport between psychology and Christianity.

Mowrer is of the opinion that abnormal behavior is caused by sin. For many years, he suggests, we have used the term "mental illness" and assumed that mental "patients" are "sick" through no fault of their own. Mowrer believes, instead, that abnormal behavior results because we have done something which society condemns and which our conscience says is wrong. I would hasten to point out, that when Mowrer talks about sin he is not thinking about something which necessarily violates divine laws. In his view, sin is limited to actions which are harmful to another person or violations of our conscience. Usually, we hide these misdeeds, lie about them, and refuse to confess them. This leads to dishonesty, and anxiety as we try to cover up.

The abnormal behavior which results from this sin can be treated in two ways. We can confess our sins to significant persons in our lives (not to God) or we can make up for the wrongs we have done. "Confession", often in groups, and "penance" thus become key words in Mowrer's system of treatment, which is known as integrity therapy.

While Bible believing Christians might be disappointed in Mowrer's refusal to acknowledge the existence and influence of a personal God, this new movement has pointed the field of psychology back to many Biblical concepts. By emphasizing the influence of sin as a cause of abnormal behavior, by recognizing that one's moral values and behavior are important in the development of abnormality, and by stressing the minister's significant role in helping the emotionally disturbed, Mowrer has focused attention on some issues which modern psychology tends to ignore. Perhaps the new interest in religion which some psychologists are showing can largely be attributed to Mowrer's influence.[14]

The Pastoral Psychology Movement

Since the time of its establishment by Christ, the church has been involved in ministering to people with personal problems. For many years the treatment of abnormal behavior was primarily the function of clergymen. But the church withdrew from this task when the term "mental illness" came into prominence and medicine took responsibility for treating people with serious personality problems. Psychology and psychiatry carried on as secular specialities and pastors began to refer those with problems to members of these new professions.

As we indicated in Chapter One, this situation began to change a few years ago. Psychologists came to recognize that religion can be an important force in the lives of their patients and pastors began to realize that psychology and psychiatry can be of help to the church. As a result the field of "pastoral psychology" began to grow significantly. Unfortunately, many pastors forgot the uniqueness of their calling, ignored the relevance of scripture and became overly impressed with psychology. They imitated psychologists to the extent that many pastors have now become "incompetent amateurs or inexpert apprentices" in the psychological arts.[15]

In spite of an over-acceptance of psychological insights and a tendency to reject scriptural truths, the pastoral psychological movement has pointed to the importance of a partnership between psychology and Christianity in treating emotional disorders. Hopefully in the future, evangelical Christians will develop a greater interest in pastoral psychology and attempt to discover how psychology and the Bible can jointly contribute to the treatment of abnormal behavior.

Does Therapy Work?

To this point we have assumed that all treatment techniques are effective in changing behavior. Is this assumption justified? Does this therapy work?

To discuss the effectiveness of psychotherapy, we must again keep in mind the threefold definition of abnormality. When a man is alienated or away from God, contemporary psychological treatment techniques will do little to meet his need. If the man is severely disturbed, psychology may bring him back into enough contact with reality that he can discuss his spiritual condition. But secular psychology cannot make new creatures out of natural men. Only God really transforms. It is the Holy Spirit who convinces men of sin, shows them their need to accept the Lordship of Jesus Christ, and guides in their subsequent spiritual maturation.

Does psychotherapy work with people who are at odds with society or at odds with themselves? The answer to this question is both "yes" and "no". If the counselee wants treatment, if the therapist has a sincere desire to help the person improve, and if there is a warm relationship between counselor and counselee, it is likely that some change in behavior will occur. The counselee will be able to get along better with other people and he may be able to overcome some of his internal frustration or resolve some of his conflicts. For these reasons, secular psychologists as well as Christian psychologists are capable of helping those who have emotional problems. Nevertheless, scripture would seem to indicate that real peace, and this would imply real emotional stability, comes not from the therapies of men but from Christ Himself.[16]

Several years ago I attended a meeting in which Dr. Mowrer presented his theoretical ideas to a group of evangelicals. When some members of the audience suggested that Christianity had the answer to men's problems, Mowrer challenged them to "prove it." Psychologists, he said are convinced not by theories, but by evidence. While we who accept scripture believe that the Word of God contains practical guidelines for meeting the problems of men, we have yet to demonstrate this to the scientific community.[17] Perhaps the greatest task facing Christian psychologists and psychiatrists is the development of effective therapeutic techniques which combine Biblical truths about man and his problems, with effective psychological "know how". Then we must show that these techniques are effective.

[1] *The reader who would like to pursue this topic further might see Robert A. Harper,* Psychoanalysis and Psychotherapy: 36 Systems. *Englewood Cliffs, New Jersey: Prentice-Hall, 1959, for a summary description of the more widely known therapy techniques.*

[2] *In* God's Psychiatry *(Westwood, New Jersey: Fleming H. Revell, 1953) Charles L. Allen has shown how the Lord's Prayer and the Beatitudes, along with the twenty-third psalm and the Ten Commandments are helpful guidelines for modern living.*

[3] *See Exodus, chapter 18. In the first chapter of his book,* Counseling for Church Leaders *(Nashville, Tennessee: Broadman, 1961), John A. Drakeford presents a concise summary of counseling situations in the Bible. In preparing this section I have leaned heavily on Dr. Drakeford's perceptive summary.*

[4] *See Exodus 18:21. "Thou shalt provide out of all the people able men, such as fear God, men of truth, hating covetousness . . ." Their availability is suggested in verse 26a "they judged the people at all seasons," and their tendency to make referrals is seen in the second part of verse 26.*

[5] *I Samuel 21:13-14.*

[6] *I Samuel 16:14-23.*

7 *Isaiah 9:6.*

8 *John 2:25.*

9 *Genesis 1:26; 9:2.*

10 *Healing is further discussed in chapter 10.*

11 *Edith Weisskopf-Joelson. "Psychology and the Insights of Religion." Paper read at First Unitarian Church, Cincinnati, Ohio, November 13, 1959. Quoted by permission.*

12 *For a further discussion of these issues see Walter D. Nunokawa,* Human Values and Abnormal Behavior. *Chicago: Scott, Foresman and Company, 1956; or Frank T. Severin,* Humanistic Viewpoints in Psychology. *New York: McGraw-Hill, 1965.*

13 *Mowrer describes the events of his life in* Abnormal Reactions or Actions? An Autobiographical Answer. *Dubuque, Iowa: Wm. C. Brown Company, 1966. Concerning his inability to assume the presidency of the psychological association, Mowrer writes "although my colleagues . . . would have been fully justified in declaring me incapacitated and installing a new president-elect directly, into office, they nevertheless installed* me *(with the past-president continuing until I was able actively to take over the duties of office) . . ."*

14 *For a further discussion of these issues, the reader might want to refer to two books by Mowrer:* The Crisis in Psychiatry and Religion. *(Princeton, New Jersey: Van Nostrand, 1961) and* The New Group Therapy. *(Princeton, New Jersey: Van Nostrand, 1964). The basic tenants of Mowrer's therapy are discussed in John W. Drakeford's book,* Integrity Therapy. *(Nashville, Tennessee: Broadman Press, 1967).*

15 *William A. Clebsch and Charles R. Jaekle,* Pastoral Care in Historical Perspective. *Englewood Cliffs, New Jersey: Prentice-Hall, 1964, p. 68.*

16 *John 14:27, 1.*

17 *The same challenge—"prove it"—should, of course, be applied to all systems of therapy. At present, very few therapies have really demonstrated their effectiveness.*

10

MIRACLES AND FAITH HEALING

The pages of the Bible are sprinkled liberally with accounts of miracles. When the Israelites were imprisoned in the land of Egypt, God instructed Moses to perform miracles that would persuade the king to release the captive nation.[1] In subsequent Jewish history, Moses, Aaron, Joshua, Samson, Samuel, Elijah, Elisha, Isaiah, Peter, Paul, and a number of apostles and disciples called upon the power of God and in so doing brought about events which were considered miraculous. Christ performed miracles — so many, in fact, that the writer of one New Testament book gave up trying to record them all.[2]

Miracles did not end when Christ ascended into heaven and the early church fathers died. From the beginning of Christianity until the present many believers have reported supernatural influences in their lives. Bernard of Clairvaux, St. Francis of Assisi, Martin Luther, George Fox, John Wesley, and more recent Christians have testified that God has worked through them to miraculously cure the sick.

For purposes of our discussion, a miracle can be defined as *an unusual event which has no natural*

*explanation but is assumed to result from the inter-
vention of some supernatural power.* In discussing the
miracles of Christ, C.S. Lewis suggested that they can
be divided into six categories.[3]

Miracles of healing refer to the events in which sick
people were made well, the blind were given sight, and
people with other infirmities were relieved of their
physical handicaps. Miracles of fertility include such
events as the changing of water into wine at the wedding feast in Cana, the feedings of the multitudes, and
the Virgin Birth of Christ.

Miracles of destruction are illustrated by the fig
tree which withered at Christ's command. Miracles of
dominion over the inorganic most often occurred at
sea and include Christ's walking upon the water and
his ability to stop storms. Miracles of reversal involve
those situations when the dead are brought back to life.
The raising of Lazarus is perhaps the best known
example. Finally, miracles of perfecting or glorifica-
tion center around the resurrection and ascension of
Christ along with the promise that all of us will some
day be raised from the dead and believers will be given
a glorious new body. In addition to these six categories,
Lewis described the coming of Christ in the form of a
man as "the grand miracle" to which all others are
related.

While a complete discussion of miracles would involve a consideration of all reported supernatural occurrences, we plan to restrict ourselves in this chapter
to the first of the categories described by Lewis.
Miracles of healing most directly concern human behavior and for this reason, they are of greatest interest
to psychology. Furthermore, although it is possible that
different kinds of miracles still occur, divine healing is
the most commonly reported form of present day
supernatural intervention. This can serve as an ex-

ample of the conflict between science and Christianity over the issue of miracles.

Examples of Faith Healing

Before considering Biblical and psychological writings about divine healing, let us look in detail at some ancient and modern examples.

In the Old Testament, the healing of Naaman is especially dramatic. Naaman was an honorable and mighty man of valor who apparently was a general in the Syrian army; but Naaman was a leper who came to the prophet Elisha and asked to be healed. After some persuasion the proud general followed Elisha's instructions and washed himself seven times in the Jordan River. As a result, the leprosy immediately disappeared and Naaman became a believer in the God of Israel.[4]

Three of the New Testament books describe how Jesus cured a man who had a withered hand. This event took place in the Temple on the Sabbath day and was the source of much subsequent discussion among the religious leaders. We have no record that the man asked to be healed but when Jesus told him to stand, he obediently arose, stretched forth his arms as instructed, and discovered that the withered hand was restored completely so that it was like his other hand.[5] It is interesting to notice that Jesus healed people with all kinds of infirmities including disease, leprosy, lameness, blindness, inability to speak, physical handicaps, fever, cuts, childhood diseases, and chronic ailments.[6]

Reports of divine healing are not limited to the Bible. In 1951 Leslie Weatherhead published a detailed case history of a four and a half year old Welsh boy named David Hughes. David had developed a disease of the kidneys. Medical examination revealed that permanent damage had been done and there was no hope for the boy's recovery. Then, a number of people began to pray. David's condition suddenly changed. Before long, his kidneys were found to be normal again and the boy was walking and running about.[7]

More startling cures of serious organic disease have been reported at shrines and faith healing meetings. While devoted believers in these methods probably report an unrealistically high number of cures, there is well documented evidence that at least some changes have taken place which reputable medical men have been unable to explain.

The Biblical Explanation

The Bible states that many miracles, including the healing of diseases, result from the presence and work of God. At the time of Jesus, it was widely accepted that the person who could perform miracles was a man of God.[8] When John the Baptist sent a little delegation to find out if Jesus was really the Messiah, Christ performed a number of miracles apparently as an expression of His divine nature.[9] The leaders in the early church and the prophets of the Old Testament all healed the sick and performed other miracles because they had been given divine power.[10]

All miracles, however, do not come from God. The Bible teaches that "signs and wonders" sometimes result from the influence of Satan and his host. These unusual events occur for the purpose of deception. While satanic power and miracles are great according to scripture, they are still minor in comparison to the power and miracles of God.[11]

Psychological Explanations

That God should intervene to bring about a change in the natural course of history is not accepted by modern man. The English philosopher David Hume once wrote that miracles are so improbable that they must be impossible. More recently, scientists (including psychologists) have concluded that miracles, like all other events, can be explained by natural causes. The most common explanations are discussed below.

1. *Miracles Reflect Inadequate Knowledge of Natural Laws*

The world in which we live is orderly. Events occur because of the operation of natural laws which science seeks to discover. Science, however, is relatively young and many of the laws of nature are still unknown. Might it be, therefore, that miracles are naturally occurring events whose causes are not understood at the time of the miracle's occurrence? Such a view would hold that the healing of Naaman was probably not a miracle at all. Perhaps the muddy waters of the Jordan River once contained some chemical which could naturally account for Naaman's immediate cure, if only we could understand the chemical laws which were operating at the time. Perhaps there is some natural explanation to account for the healing of the man with the withered hand or for the unexpected recovery of David Hughes.

This explanation of miracles is not as preposterous as it may appear at first glance. While we cannot account for the majority of miracles in the Bible, we shall see below that there are now natural explanations to account for some events which were previously considered to be completely supernatural.

One must not make the mistake, however, of assuming that we can eliminate God once we are able to logically and scientifically account for some event. Many men have concluded that as science progresses and natural laws are discovered, there will no longer be any need for God. Such a view fails to recognize that scientific progress occurs because of the permissive will of God. Rather than eliminating God, the findings of science give us further glimpses into His nature and work. Scientific progress — including that which helps us to understand some miracles — is not a memorial to the achievements of men; it is an edifice which points to the glory and power of God.

2. *Biased Reporting*

It is possible that reports of miracles and faith healing may be heavily biased. Social psychologists and students of human perception have shown that people see and believe what they want or expect to see and believe. Could it be, that miracles do not really occur except in the imagination of believers? Perhaps miracles are really misperceptions.

It is probable that reports of miraculous healings are highly exaggerated. Consider, for example, the shrine at Lourdes in Southern France. About two million pilgrims visit Lourdes every year including over 30,000 sick. It is widely believed that most of these people are cured, but careful medical studies have shown that there have been only about fifty authenticated healings.[12] On the basis of observations such as these, some writers have concluded that reports of faith healing are biased or over exaggerated and that even the so called authentic cures are the result of natural causes. It is not known whether Christian science or faith healers see a greater percentage of cures. These non-Catholic groups have been less willing than the priests at Lourdes to encourage careful studies of reported healings.

Even if the reports of success in modern faith healing are biased and exaggerated, does this say anything about the cures reported in scripture? Are these biased reports also? If the Bible is the revelation of God, it cannot be inaccurate. If we believe the Bible we must conclude that miraculous healings did and can occur apart from the biased and wishful thinking of faithful believers.

3. *The Influence of Suggestion*

Undoubtedly the most widely accepted explanation for the occurrence of faith healing is the power of suggestion. It is well known that physical illness often comes as a result of emotion and mental activity. Some physicians have suggested that over half of their patients have ailments which are psychologically caused. Apparently no part of the body is immune. The skin, the muscles, the whole respiration system, the blood and lymphatic systems, the entire digestive system, the urinary and genital parts of the body, the glands, the nervous system, the sense organs, and the heart can all be influenced by psychological pressures.

As an example of how physical illness can be psychologically caused, let us consider ulcers. This condition is usually caused by an excessive flow of acid into the stomach. This acid eats away at the lining of the stomach or intestines leaving an open wound. Since nervous tension, worry, anger, emotional strain, resentment, hostility, and anxiety are all known to increase the production of stomach acids, there is good evidence to show that these emotions, if they exist for a long period of time, can be the cause of ulcers. At one time ulcers were relatively rare but the tension of living in a modern civilization has caused this condition to be so common that physicians now estimate that about one in every ten Americans will at some time develop an ulcer.[13]

If many physical illnesses result from psychological tensions, it follows that a change in the emotional state and thinking of an individual can lead to a change in physical functioning. The best treatment for ulcers, for example, is a reduction in the anxiety which causes an oversecretion of acids in the first place.

How does this relate to faith healing? The evidence suggests that faith healers change the individual's thinking and emotional state so that there is a resulting improvement in the physical condition. When a sick person believes that he will be miraculously healed his outlook on life changes, many of the illness producing tensions disappear, the patient has a logical explanation for a fast improvement, and the admiring attention of other believers makes it no longer necessary for the patient to use the illness as a means for attracting sympathy.

Dr. Jerome D. Frank reports a number of psychological studies which show that physical changes come about because of suggestion.[14] As an example let us look at the "placebo effect." It is well known that modern drugs are very effective in treating physical ailments. It appears, however, that the mere knowledge that one is taking a drug can also bring about a change in physical condition. The taking of a harmless sugar pill is sometimes almost as effective in treating an illness as the taking of a more powerful drug. In one study, patients with bleeding ulcers were given injections of distilled water and assured that this was a new medicine which would cure them. Seventy percent showed a recovery which lasted for a period of more than a year. In another group, only twenty-five percent of the patients improved when they received the same injection but were told that this was an experimental medication of questionable value. According to Frank, harmless non-medicinal substances (usually called placebos) can relieve pain, combat anxiety, and "cure" many physiological reactions.

That much of the success of faith healing resides in the patient's state of mind was demonstrated in another interesting experimental study. Three, severely ill, bed-ridden women were treated by a prominent faith healer. One of the women had a chronic gall bladder condition, the second had failed to recuperate from a major operation and was practically a skeleton, while the third was dying from a widespread cancer. A faith healer tried to cure these patients without their knowledge. Nothing happened! Then the physician told the patients about the faith healer, built up their expectations for several days, and finally assured them that they would be treated from a distance at a certain time the next day. This was a time in which the physician was certain that the faith healer was *not* at work. At the suggested time all three patients improved quickly and dramatically. The gall bladder patient lost her symptoms, went home, and had no recurrence for several years. The second patient made a permanent recovery from her operation, while the cancer patient regained sufficient strength to go home, resume her household duties, and remain virtually symptom free until her death. According to Frank, these three patients were greatly helped by a belief — which was false — that a faith healer was treating them from a distance.[15] Obviously the patient's state of mind at the time of healing is very important. What has been called "expectant trust"[16] is, in itself, a powerful healing force.

The power of suggestion and expectant trust appears to operate in most of the more recently reported cures. The following is a lengthy but dramatic picture of what takes place when a sick person makes a pilgrimage to Lourdes. Many of the emotional reactions described below are also seen in Protestant faith healing meetings or in more private healing sessions.

Those who seek help at Lourdes have usually been sick a

long time and have failed to respond to medical reme-
dies. . . . Being chronic invalids, they have had to withdraw from most or all of their community activities and
have become burdens to their families. Their activities
have become routinized and constricted, their lives are
bleak and monotonous, and they have nothing to antici-
pate but further suffering and death.

The decision to make the pilgrimage to Lourdes changes
all this. The preparatory period is a dramatic break in
routine. Collecting funds for the journey, arranging for
medical examinations, and making the travel plans requires the co-operative effort of members of the patient's
family and the wider community. Often the congregation
contributes financial aid. Prayers and masses are offered
for the invalid. Members of the family, and often the
patient's physician or a priest, accompany him to Lourdes
and serve as tangible evidence of the interest of the family
and larger group in his welfare. Often pilgrims from
many communities travel together, and there are religious
ceremonies while the train is en route and at every stop.
In short, the preparatory period is emotionally stirring,
brings the patient from the periphery of his group to its
center, and enhances his expectation of help. It is interesting in this connection that, except for the original
cures, Lourdes has failed to heal those who live in its
vicinity. This suggests that the emotional excitement
connected with the preparatory period and journey to the
shrine may be essential for healing to occur.

On arrival at Lourdes after an exhausting, even life-
endangering journey, the sufferer's expectation of help
is further strengthened. He is plunged into "a city of
pilgrims, and they are everywhere; people who have come
from the four corners of the earth with but one purpose:
prayer, and healing for themselves or for their loved
ones. . . . One is surrounded by them, and steeped in their
atmosphere every moment of existence in Lourdes." Everyone hopes to witness or experience a miraculous cure. Accounts of previous cures are on every tongue, and the

pilgrim sees the ... offerings and the piles of discarded crutches of those who have been healed. Thus the ritual may be said to begin with a validation of the shrine's power, analogous to the medicine man's review of his cures in primitive healing rites.

The prilgrims' days are filled with religious services and trips to the Grotto, where they are immersed in the icecold spring. Every afternoon all the pilgrims and invalids who are at Lourdes at the time, and they number forty or fifty thousand, gather at the Esplanade in front of the shrine for the procession that is the climax of each day's activities. The bedridden are placed nearest the shrine, those who can sit up are behind them, the ambulatory invalids behind them, while the hordes of visitors fill the rest of the space. The enormous emotional and aesthetic impact of the procession is well conveyed by the following quotation:

At four the bells begin to peal — the Procession begins to form. The priests in their varied robes assemble at the Grotto. ... The bishop appears with the monstrance under the sacred canopy. The loud-speakers open up. A great hymn rolls out, the huge crowd joining in unison, magnificently. The Procession begins its long, impressive way down one side and up the other of the sunny Esplanade. First the Children of Mary, young girls in blue capes, white veils ... the forty or fifty priests in black cassocks ... other priests in white surplices ... then come the Bishops in purple ... and finally the officiating Archbishop in his white and gold robes under the golden canopy. Bringing up the rear large numbers of men and women of the different pilgrimages, Sisters, Nurses, members of various religious organizations; last of all the doctors. ... Hymns, prayers, fervent, unceasing. In the Square the sick line up in two rows. ... Every few feet, in front of them, kneeling priests with arms outstretched praying earnestly, leading the responses. Nurses and orderlies on their knees, praying too. ... Ardor mounts as the Blessed Sacrament approaches. Prayers gather intensity.... The Bishop leaves the shelter of the canopy, carrying the monstrance. The Sacred Host is raised above each sick one. The great crowd falls to its knees. All arms are outstretched in one vast cry to Heaven. As far as one can see in any direction, people are on their knees, praying.... [17]

Do similar suggestive influences account for the healing of the sick people who came to Jesus? It is conceivable that in some cases this was so. There are several scriptural examples of mass healings. In Mark 1, for example, Peter's mother-in-law was cured of a fever. Apparently the news of this event spread so that by evening many people were brought to Jesus for healing in what must have been an emotionally arousing situation.[18] In another instance a woman with a blood disease obviously had expectant trust and was caught up in the excitement of a jostling crowd, even though she was not anticipating that her cure would become public knowledge.[19] Since it is known that some forms of blindness, deafness, muteness, and paralysis can have psychological causes, it is conceivable that in healing people with these difficulties, Jesus was using the powerful method of suggestion.

A Possible Integration

Has psychology succeeded in explaining divine healing? Can we now eliminate the supernatural as a cause of physical cures? The Christian who believes scripture can appreciate the importance of psychological attempts to understand miracles but he must conclude that such explanations in no way eliminate the influence of God in the healing of men.

In the first place, much of the miraculous healing which is described in the Bible and some of that which has occurred subsequently cannot be explained by natural means. It is possible, of course, that at some future time such events will be explainable. At present, however, it seems very unlikely that we will ever discover natural explanations to account for the virgin birth, the resurrection of Jesus, the raising of the dead, or the immediate and permanent physical recovery of some believers. While some forms of blindness may be psychologically caused, it is unlikely that all of the blind people in scripture had this kind of a disorder — especially when the infirmity was present from birth. Scientific explanations, therefore, are not completely convincing and we must consider another approach to the miraculous.

The scriptures teach that everything was created by God through Christ. Not only were all things created through Him and for Him, but Christ also holds all things together.[20] This would suggest that God created the natural laws studied by science and that He permits them to operate. Since Christ has created everything and holds the universe together by His power, it follows that when a sick person is cured he is cured by Christ. Usually this cure comes through natural events which take place over a period of time. Harmful bacteria are over-powered or damaged tissue is repaired by the slow but orderly workings of nature. Often these cures are facilitated by drugs, by medical treatment, or by the power of suggestion. Sometimes we can explain the natural laws that are at work, but often we are baffled. In any event we can assume that God is still the prime mover causing natural events to bring about a cure. This is illustrated in figure 9-1.

On rare occasions, God apparently decides to side-step the natural processes and to bring about immediate change. When God moves in this way we say that a miracle has occurred. As an example let us consider the changing of water into wine at the wedding in Cana.

Every year, as part of the natural order, God makes wine. He does so by creating a vegetable organism that can turn water, soil, and sunlight into a juice which will, under the proper conditions, become wine. Thus, in a certain sense, he constantly turns water into wine, for wine, like all drinks, is but water modified. Once, and in one year only, God, now incarnate, short circuits the process: makes wine in a moment: uses earthenware jars instead of vegetable fibers to hold the water. But uses them to do what he is always doing. The miracle consists in the short cut; but the event to which it leads is a usual one.[21]

A similar short circuiting of nature occurred at the time of the Virgin Birth. Every child who has been conceived, except one, began life as the result of sexual intercourse. Once, however, God bypassed this natural order. He created life in the same way that all of us have been created except that the act of sexual intercourse was eliminated.

It would appear that God on occasion works in the same manner to bring about miraculous cures. Instead of proceeding through natural processes, the divine Creator sometimes repairs tissues and eliminates physically harmful influences immediately. The cure is so fast, so rare, and so inexplainable by natural laws, that we call it a miracle. Figure 9-2 illustrates how God sometimes bypasses natural causes to influence the health of men.

Some theologians have suggested that miracles are not scattered evenly over the whole course of history. Few are recorded between the time of Adam and the days of Moses. In the New Testament there are a large number of miracles but such supernatural occurrences seem relatively rare today. Perhaps it is true that miracles serve to draw attention to a new truth. Once the truths are established miracles are much less common.[22]

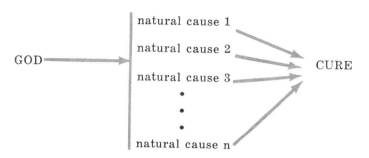

Figure 9-1. The influence of God in curing disease by working through a number of natural causes.

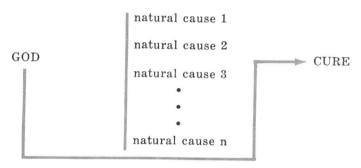

Figure 9-2. The influence of God in curing disease through miracles. On rare occasions God intervenes directly and bypasses natural causes as He cures a disease. This is a miracle.

Conclusion

Do miracles and divine healings occur in the twentieth century or are these solely events of the past? The Bible teaches that Christ is in control of all creation and that He can bring about changes in men's lives. He still heals the sick and commands us to pray for the recovery of those who are ill.[23]

It appears that God usually works through the natural laws which He has created and which modern science is discovering. It is therefore foolish to pray for recovery and then refuse medical treatment while waiting for a miracle. In most cases God heals people, not through miracles, but through medicine and the passage of time. On rare occasions God bypasses His natural laws and cures people in a supernatural way. Whether He works through natural laws which man partly understands, or through miracles which are completely beyond man's comprehension, the healing is still divine, and man must stand in awe of the sovereignty and power of God.

[1] *Exodus 7:9.*

[2] *John 20:30; 21:25.*

[3] *C. S. Lewis,* Miracles. *London: Collins Fontana Books, 1947.*

[4] *II Kings 5:1-16.*

[5] *Matthew 12:10; Mark 3:1; Luke 6:6.*

[6] *Matthew 4:23; 8:3; 16:30; Mark 1:30; Luke 22:50-51; John 4:49-50; 5:5-9.*

[7] *Leslie Weatherhead,* Psychology, Religion and Healing. *London: Hodder and Stoughton, 1951.*

[8] *John 3:2; 9:16; Acts 2:22. Sinners could not perform miracles.*

[9] *Luke 7:19-23.*

[10] *Acts 19:11; I Corinthians 12:8-10, 28.*

[11] *Miracles of the Devil are recorded in Matthew 22:24; II Thessalonians 2:9; and Revelation 13:13; 16:14; 19:20. The superiority of God's power over that of the Devil is seen in Revelation 19:20.*

[12] *Paul Meehl,* What, Then is Man? *St. Louis: Concordia Publishing House, 1958, p. 305.*

[13] *James C. Coleman,* Abnormal Psychology and Modern Life *(Third edition), Chicago: Scott, Foresman, 1964.*

[14] *Jerome D. Frank,* Persuasion and Healing. *New York: Schocken Books, 1961.*

[15] op. cit., *p. 60-61.*

[16] *This phrase is used by Frank,* op. cit., *who borrowed it from Leslie Weatherhead,* op. cit.

[17] *Jerome D. Frank,* op. cit., *pp. 64-66.*

[18] *Mark 1:29-34.*

[19] *Mark 5:25-34.*

[20] *Colossians 1:16, 17; Hebrews 1:2-3.*

[21] *C. S. Lewis,* op. cit., *p. 140.*

[22] *A. H. Strong,* Systematic Theology. *Westwood, New Jersey: Fleming H. Revell, 1907, p. 128.*

[23]*James 5:13-15.*

11

PREACHING, BRAINWASHING, AND BEHAVIOR MANIPULATION

Before ascending to heaven, Jesus met with His followers and told them that they were to become His witnesses throughout the world.[1] The early Christians sought to fulfill this "great commission," and faithful believers have been Christ's witnesses ever since.

To be a witness for Christ appears to involve at least three overlapping activities: preaching, conversion, and teaching. On a number of occasions Jesus instructed his disciples to *preach* and in the book of Mark the last recorded speech of Christ begins with the phrase "go ye into all the world and preach."[2] The purpose of such preaching was that men might experience *conversion* and become followers of Christ.[3] In addition, Christ indicated that his followers should *teach* others about Him and His commandments.[4] In this chapter and the two which follow we will consider how psychology relates to preaching, conversion, and teaching in the local church.

According to the American College Dictionary, to preach is to advocate religious or moral truth in speech or writing, to proclaim the Gospel or make it known by a sermon, and to give earnest advice on religious subjects. The dictionary adds that this is sometimes done in "an obtrusive or tedious way."[5]

Is preaching effective in changing behavior and causing conversion? Some psychologists have studied evangelistic preaching in an attempt to answer this question. One researcher, for example, has concluded that evangelistic meetings

... are characterized by high emotional intensity. Before the evangelist comes to town, there may be a preliminary build-up through publicity and sermons, which creates some anticipatory excitement, arouses latent feelings of guilt, and holds out the hope of relief through salvation. The meetings themselves are highly emotional. The impact of the dramatic pleas, threats, and exhortations of the evangelist may be intensified through the singing of highly emotional gospel hymns by the entire audience, led by a choir and soloist....

The revivalist tries to arouse feelings of sin, guilt, and fear in his hearers by harping on their wickedness and the dire punishments that await those who do not repent. At the same time he dwells on the bliss that awaits them if they confess their sins, ask God's forgiveness, and mend their ways.[6]

This writer goes on to describe the characteristics of a successful evangelistic preacher. He should have "a deep religious conviction, a capacity for vivid, intense emotional experiences, which he can successfully communicate to others, sensitivity to audience response ... great organizational ability, (and) personal prestige."[7] While preaching in a large meeting can influence almost anybody, the study concluded that people who respond are most often economically or socially underprivileged, extroverts, or persons with low opinions of themselves.

Perhaps one of the harshest psychological appraisals of preaching came in a book which appeared in 1957. In this volume the author skillfully argued that evangelistic preaching techniques are similar to the brainwashing methods used by Communists behind the Iron Curtain.[8]

If evangelistic preaching is the same as brainwashing, we have surely deviated from the last commands of Jesus. But *is* mass evangelism really a form of brainwashing? Are Christians who support the preaching of men like Billy Graham actually giving encouragement to an unethical manipulation of human behavior? Are we inconsistent if we condemn Communist brain-washing but support mass evangelism? To answer these questions we must understand the basic principles of Communist brainwashing.

The Nature of Brainwashing

In 1953 a psychologist interviewed several American prisoners of war immediately after they had been released from North Korean prison camps.[9] These interviews revealed that Communist brainwashing involves three steps: creating a breakdown, providing an answer, and consolidating new beliefs.

Creating a Breakdown

The Communists created a breakdown in two ways. First, there was physical hardship. In Korea, once the prisoners were captured, they were subjected to a long march north. Most of the time they were cold, poorly fed, tired, foot-sore, and without sufficient clothing. When they finally arrived at the prison camp they discovered that there was no place to wash or shave, food was poor, toilet facilities were terrible, and the conditions were so crowded that nine men were forced to live in each of the 12' by 12' rooms.

Along with these physical hardships there was psychological indoctrination. The prison officials cut off the inmates' contact with the outside world. Newspapers were not provided, letters were withheld or censored, and routines were disrupted so that the prisoner never really knew what to expect next. There were long lectures and discussions on Communism, and prisoners sometimes would be questioned day and night with the persistent demand that they "confess to their 'crimes'." Since secret spies were thought to be in the camp reporting on the prisoners' behavior, the inmates began to distrust everyone, including their former buddies. Before long, men began to doubt the value of United Nations involvement in Korea. As the strain continued, many began to look down on themselves and to acknowledge that they were "no good." Eventually, some of the prisoners broke down, often in dramatic ways.

The crisis usually starts with hysteria and sobbing at night, which go on during the small group meeting the next day and are immediately discussed. . . . The crisis usually comes at about the same time for all the members of a small group. Apparently the breakdown of one of the members launches a chain reaction. . . . In some cases, of course, it is much more evident than in others. The cynics and those with a sense of humor seem to survive best. . . . It is usually during this acute crisis and breakdown that what the Chinese aptly call 'tail cutting' takes place: 'the "tails" are ties with the old society such as family, friends, old values, and so forth'.[10]

Providing an Answer

Having rejected the "old life" the prisoner is willing to accept the answers of Communism. He embraces the Communist beliefs, learns the language, and becomes convinced that he must publicize his newly found faith so that others may find peace of mind through accepting the Communist doctrines.

Consolidating the New Beliefs

The Communists discovered that the new converts were not very faithful unless the change in thought was sustained by subsequent group discussions and other kinds of emotional support. Although the converts were required to attend frequent Communist meetings, they were treated kindly, awarded special privileges, given status in the form of special badges on their uniforms, and promised a better life in the future. Underlying all of this, however, was an implied threat that things would be much worse should the convert change his mind and decide to return to his old ways.

It must not be assumed that all prisoners of war were successfully brainwashed. Less than fifteen percent of the prisoners in Korean detention camps collaborated with the enemy. When the war was over and prisoners were given their freedom, only a few chose to remain in Communist China. Of these, several later rejected the Communist way of life and returned home.

Is Preaching a Form of Brainwashing?

Psychologists who have been critical of preaching have suggested that in evangelistic meetings, as in brainwashing, there is a breakdown, answer, and consolidation stage.

Creating a Breakdown

The evangelist, of course, does not create physical hardship in order to break down his potential convert. But there are other ways of controlling an individual so that he becomes susceptible to a persuasive message. Research has demonstrated that people are more suggestible when they are in a crowd and when strong emotion is aroused. Usually, preachers try to attract large crowds and there is sometimes an attempt to stir up emotion in the congregation. Frequently, the speaker repetitiously reminds his audience that they are sinners. This leads to feelings of guilt accompanied by fear. Jonathan Edwards in one of his sermons was very dramatic in creating horror in his audiences. "The God that holds you over the pit of hell, much as we hold a spider, or some loathsome insect over the fire, abhors you, and is dreadfully provoked. His wrath towards you burns like fire."[11] Slowly such preachers build up anxiety and fear over the future. The enthusiastic response of other believers and the emotional impact of music combine to create mental exhaustion in the potential convert. Eventually, like the prisoner in the Communist camp, there are no more defences. The hearer is willing to cut ties with his old life and embrace the answer of the preacher.

Providing an Answer

The message of the preacher varies somewhat with his brand of theology. Most evangelists, however, encourage potential converts to repent, be saved, and accept Christ into their lives. They are told that by doing this their lives will be different. They are assured of eternal life in heaven and an abundant life on earth. Many people who respond, soon learn the religion's jargon and become enthusiastic about converting others to their new-found faith.

Consolidating the New Beliefs

As with the prisoners who are persuaded by brainwashing, the number of people who respond to preaching tends to be relatively small. Even those who report a conversion sometimes turn away from their new-found faith unless they are given considerable support and encouragement by other believers. Church groups, therefore, often receive the evangelist's converts willingly. The importance of prayer and Bible reading — which might be considered as a form of continued indoctrination — is emphasized. Like the Communists who are encouraged to liberate the world, the religious convert is encouraged to be a witness of his new-found faith and there are implied threats about what will happen if the convert decides to return to his old way of life.

It cannot be denied that the events which take place in a large preaching meeting and the events which occur in a brainwashing situation are very similar. Undoubtedly many preachers *do* use psychological techniques — usually in innocence — to persuade men to change their religious beliefs. As a result of this preaching people sometimes do appear to be "won" as "converts." It is more likely, however, they have been manipulated by gimmicks similar to those used by the brainwashers, and the man who is won by a gimmick is seldom really converted. It is not surprising that he "falls away."

In spite of the similarities there are also differences between preaching and brainwashing.[12] For example a preacher whose ministry is guided by the directives of the New Testament does not rely on tricks to convert men. He realizes that it is not clever human devices, but the power of the Holy Spirit that convicts men of sin and convinces them of their need for Christ. The preacher's job is to proclaim the good news as he is led by the Holy Spirit. The hearer's freedom to accept or reject the gospel message must always be respected. In contrast, the brainwashers make no claims to divine guidance and they care little about respecting individual freedom. Of course most non-Christian psychologists would reject these distinctions. They would say that the preacher and brainwasher use methods which *look* the same in spite of the preacher's stated respect for individual freedom and claims of divine guidance.

There are, however, other less theological differences between preaching and brainwashing. First, brainwashing is basically emotional and few people are convinced rationally. When the emotional impact wears off the convert returns to his old way of life. Now it cannot be denied that there is considerable emotion in many preaching meetings but when the emotion dies down, there are many people whose lives have been permanently changed. Permanent changes following brainwashing are almost non-existent. Secondly, brainwashing always involves group pressure. Sometime people are converted to Christianity while under the influence of groups but many times individuals are alone at the time of conversion. The persuasive effect of some past sermon may have long disappeared and the individual is converted without even thinking about group influences. This would never be true of brainwashing. Thirdly, unlike the brainwasher, the preacher does not create physical hardships with a promise of a later reduction in physical stress. Indeed, if the preacher is true to the Word of God he must tell his audience that becoming a Christian might *create* hardships rather than reduce them. It is often much easier to stay as you are and not become a believer. Fourthly, cynics or intellectuals almost never change as a result of brainwashing. While these people are also less likely to be influenced by preaching,[14] it is nevertheless true that a number do come to Christ. Paul's sermon on Mars Hill is an example of preaching which resulted in conversion among scholars.

There are some techniques of communication which everyone uses. Counselors, politicians, and teachers, as well as preachers and brainwashers use many similar methods. The fact that some people misuse the techniques of communication does not make the techniques bad in themselves any more than the misuse of guns or drugs makes these inventions bad. It should also be remembered that psychologists who have criticized preaching have focused their attention on large evangelistic meetings. Most preaching however, takes place in smaller groups where the psychological pressures are usually less intense. Such situations bear little resemblance to brainwashing.

Although few Christians are likely to agree with modern psychologists who claim that preaching is really a form of brainwashing, we can be grateful for the insight that such psychological thinking has provided. We are now better able to understand some of the techniques which the Holy Spirit uses to change men's lives. More important, these insights can prevent us from developing an over-dependence on gimmicks or uncontrolled imagination and can stimulate preachers to rely on the guiding control of the Holy Spirit.

Behavior Manipulation

There are differences between preaching and brainwashing but both seek to manipulate and control the thinking and activities of other people. Most of the preaching in the Bible and much of the reported conversation between individuals was an attempt by one person to change the behavior of others. Is such behavior control possible? Is it morally right? The whole topic of the control and manipulation of human behavior has received considerable study from psychologists and other scientists within the past few years.

In considering this issue it must be recognized that our whole society is involved in behavior control. The advertiser tries to manipulate the behavior of potential buyers. The politician tries to sway the behavior of others. The parent attempts to control the behavior of his children. The college professor is involved in the manipulation of students and students, in turn, are often very successful in manipulating the behavior of professors. Clearly modern man is both manipulating and manipulated.

It would be surprising if Christians remained aloof from this widespread human activity. Like everybody else, pastors, Christian education directors, missionaries, Sunday school teachers, church leaders, and those who are in the pews are all involved in manipulating other people and being manipulated. Indeed, the work of the church is primarily concerned with changing people's actions. We want, for example, to bring men who are unsaved to a knowledge of Jesus Christ. We want to assist the believer so that he can grow in his faith and live a purposeful, spiritual life. We want to train Christians so that they, as individuals can study the Word of God and spread the Gospel through effective witnessing.

Throughout history, man's attempts to control the behavior of other men have not always been successful. In recent years modern science has studied this problem carefully and demonstrated that we can alter behavior with a high degree of efficiency. Dr. Carl Rogers, a past President of the American Psychological Association, gave a speech a few years ago in which he discussed the control of behavior. In his speech he summarized some of the facts which psychologists have learned about the control of behavior.

We know how to set up conditions under which many members of a group will report judgments which are contrary to the evidence of their senses.

We know a great deal about how to establish conditions

which will influence consumer responses and/or public opinion.

We know how to influence the buying behavior of individuals by setting up conditions which provide satisfaction for needs of which they are unconscious, but which we have been able to determine.

We know how to predict which members of an organization will be troublesome and delinquent.

We know how to provide conditions in a work group, whether in industry or in education, which will be followed by increased productivity, originality, and morale.

We know how to provide the conditions of leadership which will be followed by personality growth in the members of the group, as well as by increased productivity and improved group spirit.

We know how to provide the psychological conditions in the classroom which will result not only in unusual learning of academic content, but in improved personal adjustment as well.

We know how to provide an interpersonal relationship with qualities such that it enables the individual to meet stress with more serenity, less anxiety.

We know the attitudes which, if provided by a counselor or a therapist, will be predictably followed by certain constructive personality and behavior changes in the client.

We know how, I believe, to disintegrate a man's personality structure, dissolving his self-confidence, destroying the concept he has of himself, and making him completely dependent upon another.

We know how to provide psychological conditions which will produce vivid hallucinations and other abnormal reactions in the thoroughly normal individual in the waking state.

We know how to influence psychological moods, attitudes, and behaviors through drugs.

We know the psychological conditions of family life which, if established in a home, will tend to produce emotionally secure children with many socially valuable characteristics.[15]

On the basis of these conclusions and a significant amount of research which has been done since Rogers gave his speech, it can be accurately stated that behavior can be and is being effectively manipulated.

This realization should cause concerned Christians to ask at least two questions. First we must ask whether or not psychologists and other scientists are able to prevent unethical people from using these techniques to serve their own selfish ends. Secondly, we must question the extent to which such techniques can be or should be used in the work of the local church. Let us consider each of these questions in turn.

Control of Manipulation Techniques

In our complex society some control of human behavior is inevitable. The government, the economy, and the social expectations of the culture all exert a control which is necessary if we are going to survive as a civilization. But the ability to manipulate men can have both good and bad results. The control of behavior, permits men to become more happy and productive but there is also a danger that we will become the slaves of some power-mad despot. Since man is by nature evil, we really can't be certain that the techniques of manipulation will not be misused. Nevertheless, psychologists have suggested at least four ways by which man can prevent the misuse of these powers.

1. Psychologists can conduct research into the methods by which behavior can be manipulated. This

knowledge will enable us to better understand and control the manipulation techniques.

2. Psychologists can keep the general public informed about ways in which people are controlled. If people know how they can be manipulated, they are less likely to be controlled against their will and they are less likely to be influenced by sensation-seeking writers. It has already been shown by psychological experiments that awareness of the manipulator's goals and techniques is a good way for a person to avoid being manipulated.

3. We can all learn more about ourselves — our needs, our values, our strengths, our weaknesses and our emotions. People cannot be manipulated easily if they know more about themselves than does the would-be manipulator.

4. We can develop a genuine and spontaneous honesty. According to one psychologist the manipulator is characterized by deception and dishonesty. He uses tricks and clever maneuvers to control others and cannot function if people express their feelings and ideas about him. "A major defense against manipulation would be for the rest of us to learn to become *honestly* expressive of our own ideas."[16]

To this list we might add a fifth alternative. If the nature of man can be changed so that he is under the control of the Holy Spirit he will not be involved in manipulating other people for selfish motives. Such a change in nature comes only through a realization of man's need for Christ and his decision to invite Christ to control his life. This was the message that Jesus left for his disciples to preach after He went back to heaven.

Behavior Manipulation in the Church

Is it right to use manipulation techniques in the

church? Should we be using some of these techniques, for example, in world evangelism? Recently a number of scientists, many of whom were Christians, met to discuss this question. In the middle of the meeting a lady got up and asked "I would like to know if it would be all right to drug people and while they're under the influence of drugs to convince them that they should become Christians?"

Difficult questions such as this rarely have simple solutions. It has already been suggested however, that we cannot trick or psychologically manipulate a person into accepting Christ or into growing spiritually. It is the Holy Spirit, and not a psychological technique, which works in men's lives to convict them of sin and to lead them into spiritual maturity.

While thoughtful Christians may disagree, it is the author's opinion that we in the church are free to use any manipulation technique if (1) we do so prayerfully and with a sincere desire to be led by the Holy Spirit, and (2) we respect the right of men to make their own decisions. At no place in scripture does Jesus or any other servant of God force men to change their behavior. I agree with the President of Moody Bible Institute who, in a few words, summarizes the attitude which Christians should have when they consider the use of psychological manipulation techniques in the church.

I shall respect each man's right to his faith or even lack of it. Lut that does not mean that I shall not attempt to convert him. I'll oppose any attempt to coerce him, or force him by physical or other means to a decision against his will. For I believe God wants only the glad hearted willing surrender of the heart to himself.[17]

[1] *Acts 1:4, 8.*

2 *Mark 16:15. Some modern versions do not include Mark 16:1-20, but this does not alter the fact that Jesus expected his followers to preach. See Matthew 10:7; 27; Luke 9:20, 60.*

3 *Matthew 28:19-20 reads in part "make disciples of all nations." Mark 16:15-16 implies that the preaching was for the purpose of leading men to believe in Christ so that they would be saved.*

4 *Matthew 28:19-20 makes two references to the importance of teaching.*

5 *C. L. Barnhart (Editor),* The American College Dictionary. *New York: Random House, 1962, p. 952.*

6 *Jerome D. Frank.* Persuasion and Healing. *New York: Schocken Books, 1961, pp. 77-78.*

7 op. cit., *p. 79.*

8 *William Sargant,* Battle for the Mind. *London: Pan Books, 1957. Quoted by permission.*

9 *Edgar H. Schein, Reaction patterns to severe chronic stress in American Army Prisoners of war of the Chinese.* Journal of Social Issues, *vol. 13, 1957, pp. 56-60.*

10 *Sargant,* op. cit., *p. 150.*

11 *J. A. C. Brown,* Techniques of Persuasion: From Propaganda to Brainwashing. *Baltimore: Penguin, 1963, p. 231.*

12 *Much of the following discussion is guided by the thinking of Dr. Martyn Lloyd-Jones, whose booklet* Conversions: Psychological and Spiritual *(London: Inter-Varsity Press, 1959) is an answer to Sargant,* op. cit.

13 *Acts 2:6-12.*

14 *I Corinthians 1:26.*

15 *Carl Rogers. "Implications of Recent Advances in Prediction and Control of Behavior."* Teachers College Record, *57, 1956, pp. 316-322.*

16 *Everett L. Shostrom,* Man, the Manipulator. *Nashville: Abingdon, 1967. The quotation is from pages 69-70.*

17 *Quoted in a sermon delivered during the 1967 Founders Week Conference by William Culbertson, Moody Bible Institute, Chicago, Illinois.*

12

CONVERSION

Early in the twentieth century, an American psychologist named William James travelled to Scotland where he gave a series of lectures. Based on a study of diaries, personal letters, confessions, and testimonies, James had reached a number of conclusions about the psychology of conversion and other religious experiences. These conclusions were presented in the lectures and later published in what was to become an influential book on the psychology of religion.[1]

Since the appearance of James' book, there have always been a few psychologists with an interest in conversion and in the psychological changes that follow religious experience. In this chapter we will summarize some psychological views of conversion and compare them with Biblical statements.

Psychological Views of Conversion

According to one dictionary definition, religious conversion involves a change from one religion to another which is regarded as better. The change includes an alteration of character in which a person turns from an evil or sinful form of life to a righteous one.[2]

When psychologists began a careful study of religious experience they concluded that the dictionary definition was too simple. Conversion, it was agreed, must be defined with greater precision. To do this, the psychologist has had to consider at least four questions.

1. Is conversion gradual or sudden? William James was of the opinion that conversion could be *either* a gradual developing process or an event which occurred suddenly at a point in time. Other psychologists suggested that conversion was *both* gradual and sudden. They assumed that in every case there is a gradual change in thinking which eventually causes one to experience sudden conversion. Still other psychologists have taken a position for one side of this question or the other. Some view conversion as being always an abrupt change in behavior while others claim that conversion is always a slow process.

2. Is conversion unconscious and involuntary or is it conscious and voluntary? Some psychologists have concluded that unconscious influences can lead to religious conversions which the converts cannot voluntarily control. This is different from the view which says that conversions are primarily conscious and a result of the convert's voluntary decision. Closely related to this is the question of whether conversion is mainly an intellectual decision or an emotional response to stimulation.

3. Does conversion result in growth or deterioration? William James thought that conversion was primarily good. In his view, the convert changed from a condition of being "divided, consciously wrong, inferior and unhappy," to a state of being "unified, consciously right, superior and happy." Later, other psychologists began to question whether conversion always brought a change for the good and at least one writer

concluded that there must be two kinds of conversions: those which cause the individual to mature into a psychologically healthier person and those which cause him to regress to a state of increased anxiety and psychological maladjustment.[3]

4. Is conversion a natural or supernatural event? This question, which might seem of greatest importance to the Christian, is usually ignored by psychologists. Psychology is a science which seeks to understand behavior. Although it may recognize the possibility of external, supernatural influences, psychology correctly assumes that the study of these influences is beyond the reach of scientific techniques. As a result, psychologists usually work on the assumption that religious experiences have natural explanations and that there is no need to become concerned about the influence of God or any other supernatural individual.

These disagreements over the definition and nature of conversion have hindered the psychological study of religious experience.[4] Currently, there is no one psychological view to explain conversion. Instead, psychologists have proposed several theories, including the following: conversion is a response to group pressure, a reaction in adolescence, or an experience of psychological integration.[5]

Conversion as a response to group pressure

Some authors believe that conversion "takes place in the high-voltage atmosphere of an evangelistic service, a service marked by semi-hypnotic suggestibility, unbridled irrationality and surging emotionalism. . . . The conversion-experience has nothing supernatural about it. Mass-excitement explains the decisions that are reached."[6] This view has been most dramatically stated by the English psychiatrist William Sargant who regards all conversions — political as well as

religious — as a result of "temporarily impaired judg-
ment and a heightened suggestibility" that occurs in
large group situations especially if these are characterized by fear, anger, or excitement.[7] Sargant suggests that there are striking similarities between re-
vival meetings, voodoo dances, snake handling services,
shock treatment, drug reactions, and psychological con-
ditioning.

Conversion as an adolescent reaction

The early teenage years are times of physical change
and psychological pressure. The young adolescent must
throw over his childish ways and learn to act like an
adult. All of this can be frustrating and discouraging.
It is during these difficult years that the greatest number of religious conversions occur. Can we assume
that the pressures of adolescence temporarily over-
whelm the individual and make him especially open
to the "good news" of religion? Some psychologists
have answered "yes" and concluded with William
James that conversion is primarily a normal reaction
to the stress of adolescence.[8]

Conversion ... is a normal phase of adolescence in every
class of human beings. The age is the same, falling usually between fourteen and seventeen. The symptoms are
the same — a sense of incompleteness and imperfection;
brooding, depression; morbid introspection, and sense of
sin; anxiety about the hereafter; distress over doubts,
and the like. And the result is the same — a happy relief
and objectivity. ... Conversion is in its essence a normal
adolescent phenomenom, incidental to the passage from
the child's small universe to the wider intellectual and
spiritual life of maturity.[9]

This view assumes that conversion is an experience
which enables young people to find meaning in life and
to grow up more quickly. Presumably similar psycho-

logical development could occur without conversion but such development would be much slower.

Conversion as psychological integration

This position regards conversion as occurring in three steps. First, there occurs a sense of perplexity, uneasiness, and awareness of sin accompanied by an intense dissatisfaction with one's self. When the individual is overwhelmed by these feelings of worthlessness he reaches the second stage of conversion — the stage of self surrender and turning. At this point he recognizes his need to accept the answers and support provided by the newly discovered religion. Third, is a state of relaxation, a release from tension, and the experience of joy, peace, and happiness.[10] All of this suggests that when a person is converted he finds psychological meaning and integration in place of a disrupted, unhappy, problem-filled life.

These three psychological views of conversion are the most widely held but there are other theories. Some have suggested that conversion is primarily an expression of psychological instability. Others believe that true conversion only comes late in life. Some hold the opinion that conversion is the result of conflicts with parents and other authority figures. More recently there has been widespread return to an old view that religious experiences involve solitary contemplation and sensory experience. LSD and other drugs are assumed to provide experiences similar to those of a religious convert.

Obviously, psychological considerations of conversion are not limited to Christian religious experience. Conversion to a new political belief or non-Christian religion is assumed to have some of the same elements that have been described above.

Biblical Views of Conversion

The Bible appears to support the following conclusions about Christian conversion.

Christian conversion occurs at a specific point in time

The decision to personally accept Jesus Christ as Saviour and to commit one's life to his Lordship occurs at a moment in time. In the original Greek language, John 3 and I Peter 1:3 described the new birth in a tense which indicates an instant occurrence.[11]

While Christian conversion is instantaneous, the act is often preceded by a period of struggle, hesitancy, deliberation, and conviction. Following the conversion decision there is a life-long period of continued growth and spiritual development. Sometimes the pre-conversion deliberation and the post-conversion growth fuse together so that the convert cannot remember his moment of decision. This can create the impression that conversion is gradual when in fact it is instantaneous.

Christian conversion experiences differ from person to person

The conversion experience occurs in different ways and results in a variety of psychological manifestations.[12] All of us have different characteristics. As a result we show diversified reactions to religious experiences just as we react differently to non-religious events. For some people, conversion comes after a long intellectual deliberation. Others respond following a brief sermon. For some, conversion is accompanied by crying and other emotional behavior. For others, there are no such emotional expressions. Many people experience conversion when they are in the presence of a group. Others are alone when they respond. Some people accept Christ when they are adolescents but many others are converted when they are children or adults. For some, conversion is the event which provides the answer to all of life's problems. For others, this religious experience is only the beginning of a series of questions and uncertainties. One need only consider the conversions of Paul, Nicodemus, the multitude who heard Peter preach on the day of Pentecost, the Philippian jailor, the Ethiopian eunuch, Lydia the saleslady, and the Bible students at Berea to recognize that there are great individual differences in the way in which people come to Christ.[13]

Christian conversion is voluntary and conscious

The Bible gives no support to the view that one can be converted involuntarily and without being conscious of his decision. Christian conversion involves a conscious belief in the divinity of Jesus Christ, a deliberate decision to confess and forsake one's sinful ways, and a voluntary receiving of Christ as the Lord of one's life.[14]

Christian conversion is supernatural

A person can be converted to a political doctrine or religion without the intervention of any supernatural being. The Bible clearly states that anyone who is converted to Christ becomes a "new creature" as the result of divine intervention. This transformation of life is a gift from God.[15]

Christian conversion brings the potential for a complete change in behavior

When a person is converted to Christ there can be a change in his characteristic ways of behaving. This is seen in several Biblical examples. Peter, the profane fisherman became a man of great spiritual power and concern for other people. John, a vindictive person, became an apostle of love. Saul, the fanatic persecutor of Christians became a tender-hearted follower of Jesus Christ. The cold-hearted jailor of Philippi became a sympathetic friend.[16] All of these people, and many since, were changed for the better because Christ altered their lives.

Christian conversion can lead to a changed emotional outlook so that the believer experiences love, joy, and peace. His personality can alter so that he is relatively free of jealousy or hard feelings and characterized instead by patience, kindness, goodness, faithfulness, gentleness, and self-control. His values may change and a gradual alteration in his worldview occurs. The Christian sees at least some things from God's perspective.[17]

It is not inevitable that such positive benefits result from Christian conversion. Several years ago a psychiatric study of religious converts showed that some people develop an irrational intensity of belief in their new doctrine, a contemptuous hatred for the old belief, intolerance for anyone who does not believe like the convert, a crusading zeal which attempts to force others to become converts, and an unhealthy need for martyrdom and self-punishment.[18] According to this psychiatric report, religious conversion can lead to hatred, intolerance, and irrational behavior. In scripture, Ananias and Sapphira, John Mark in his early years as a believer, and Demas were people whose conversions were apparently genuine but whose behavior did not change for the better.[19]

It appears, therefore, that while every Christian convert has the potential for personality change, for some the potential is never realized. Some Christians do not show better dispositions, develop a happier outlook on life, experience the disappearance of all problems, or develop healthier personalities because they have accepted Christ.

In conversion new life is supernaturally begotten, yet that new life does not unfold magically, automatically, spontaneously. That new life must be assiduously cultivated by teaching, fellowship and discipline. . . . The potential for personality-change rarely occurs except within a context of helpful fellowship and spiritual discipline. Ignore the human factors and the divine potential remains dormant.[20]

For change to occur in the life of a Christian convert, the Holy Spirit must work either directly in the believer's yielded life, or indirectly through the ministry of other committed believers.[21]

Conclusion

There is considerable similarity between conversions which are Christian and those which are not Christian. Many of the same psychological events which take place in religious and political conversions also occur when a person commits his life to Christ. Because of these similarities it is possible for an individual to show evidence of conversion even though he has not experienced the new birth about which the Bible speaks.

Psychological studies can explain what takes place when one has a religious experience but psychology cannot account for the change which takes place when an individual commits himself to Christ. All conversion experiences show similar psychological characteristics but that which makes Christian conversion different from all others is the person of Christ.[22] The Bible does not say that if any man be converted he is a new creature. Instead, we read that "if a man is *in Christ* he becomes a new person altogether — the past is finished and gone, everything has become fresh and new."[23] To spread this good news and to see men converted to Christ is the task which Jesus gave to the church before ascending into heaven many years ago.

[1] *William James.* Varieties of Religious Experiences: A Study in Human Nature. *Garden City, New York: Dolphin Books, Doubleday & Company, Inc., 1902.*

[2] *C. L. Barnhart (Editor)* The American College Dictionary. *New York: Random House, 1962.*

[3] *Leon Salzman, Types of Religious Conversion.* Pastoral Psychology, *17, September 1966, pp. 8-20, 66.*

[4] *For a further discussion of the problems of definition, see Earl H. Furgeson, The Definition of Conversion,* Pastoral Psychology, *16, September 1965, pp. 8-16.*

5 *Vernon Grounds, Psychiatry and Christianity: Conversion.* His, *24, November 1963, pp. 26-31, 34.*

[6] Ibid., *p. 26.*

[7] *William Sargant,* Battle For the Mind. *London: Pan Books, 1957, p. 128.*

[8] *For additional and more complete discussions of this topic, see: Carl W. Christensen, Religious Conversion in Adolescence,* Pastoral Psychology, *16, September 1965, pp. 17-28; Charles W. Stewart, The Religious Experience of Two Adolescent Girls,* Pastoral Psychology, *17, September 1966, pp. 49-55; and Charles W. Stewart,* Adolescent Religion. *Nashville: Abingdon, 1967.*

[9] *James, op. cit., p. 185.*

[10] *Edward Scribner Ames, Stages in Religious Conversion. In Orlo Strunk, Jr. (Editor)* Readings in the Psychology of Religion. *New York: Abingdon, 1959, pp. 140-143.*

[11] *Robert O. Ferm,* The Psychology of Christian Conversion. *Westwood, New Jersey: Fleming H. Revell, 1959. See especially pages 171-175.*

[12] Ibid., *p. 214.*

[13] *These conversions are reported in Acts 9; John 3; Acts 2; 16:25-34; 8:26-39; 16:14-15; 17:10-12.*

[14] *John 3:16, 36; 5:24; Romans 10:9, 10; Isaiah 55:7; Acts 2:38; John 1:12.*

[15] *II Corinthians 5:17; 9:15; Galatians 6:15; Ephesians 2:8-9; Romans 6:23.*

[16] *Acts 12:15; Luke 9:53-54; I John 4:7; Acts 9:1; 16:24, 33; 21:13.*

[17] *Galatians 5:22-23, 26; I Corinthians 2:15-16; II Corinthians 5:17.*

[18] *Salzman,* op. cit., *pp. 18-19.*

[19] *Acts 5:1-10; 15:38; II Timothy 4:10.*

[20] *Vernon Grounds, Psychiatry and Christianity: Conversion, Part 2.* His, *24, December 1963, pp. 39-40. Reprinted by permission.*

[21] *Ephesians 5:18; Galatians 5:16-25 show the direct influence of the Holy Spirit in a life. At the time of his conversion, Paul was influenced by the Holy Spirit through the ministry of Ananias (Acts 9). Later Paul was the Holy Spirit's vehicle to bring changes in the lives of the early Christians.*

[22] *Ferm,* op. cit., *p. 225.*

[23] *I Corinthians 5:17, Phillips.*

13

PSYCHOLOGY AND CHRISTIAN TEACHING

How do people learn?

What is the best way to teach?

These questions are far older than the science of psychology. The ancient Egyptians believed that the best teaching was accompanied by punishment. The Greeks and subsequent generations of teachers, accepted this theory and beat their children with canes in an attempt to stimulate learning. Later, these more brutal forms of punishment were replaced by ridicule, scolding, sarcasm, criticism, detention, withdrawal of privileges, extra homework, and a number of other devices which controlled the student's behavior but probably did little to facilitate learning. More recently, brightly painted classrooms, friendly teachers, field trips, and the use of such mechanical devices as films, tape recorders, or television have all been used to increase the effectiveness of education. In spite of these significant advances, much teaching is still ineffective and most children prefer Saturdays and summer vacations to days in school.

It should come as no surprise that children who do not like day school carry their dislike to Sunday school. Teachers in church schools are often untrained, poorly prepared, and without enthusiasm. The Sunday school frequently lacks good audio-visual techniques and cannot use the day school's methods of controlling behavior. As a result, Sunday school students tend to be disinterested, bored, and inclined to drop out as soon as there is a let-up in parental pressure to attend.

The weaknesses and inefficiencies of both public schools and Sunday schools have been widely reported. Many qualified experts in the field of education — including Christian Education — have analyzed and tried to overcome these weaknesses. The result has been a continuing improvement in both the techniques and effectiveness of teaching.

In these attempts to understand and improve education, the science of psychology has played an important role. Literally thousands of experiments have been carried out on the topic of learning. These studies have shown that learning is very complex but that teaching could be more efficient in secular and Sunday school classrooms.

Psychological Experiments in Learning

The best known learning experiments have been done in the laboratories of Dr. B. F. Skinner, a Harvard University psychologist who works with pigeons. Skinner designed a special learning cage on one wall of which was a little round disk where the pigeon could peck. Under the disk was a window through which food could be given to the bird (see figure 13-1). Skinner called this food "reinforcement." He found that by giving or withholding reinforcement, pigeons could be taught such actions as turning in circles or distinguishing between different colors and shapes. Since Skinner's original work in 1930, many other psychologists have shown how the presentation of reinforcement can be used to mold the behavior of rats, mice, turtles, monkeys, fish, cats, dogs, and a variety of other animals. The seal act in a circus is a well known example of behavior which has been taught by the use of reinforcement. The animal balances a ball on his nose because he has learned that this performance will be reinforced subsequently with a piece of fish.

On the basis of Skinner's work and that of his students, a number of learning principles have been firmly established. A few of these principles are as follows:

1. As long as an animal is given reinforcement he will continue indefinitely with the behavior for which he is reinforced. If a pigeon is given reinforcement for pecking a disk, he'll continue to peck. If he is given reinforcement for turning around in the cage, he'll continue to turn around. If a seal is given reinforcement for balancing a ball, he'll continue to respond to the ball by balancing it on his nose.

2. Reinforcement speeds up learning. It is possible to learn without being reinforced, but this is very slow and inefficient.

3. If reinforcement stops, behavior eventually disappears. When Skinner's pigeons were no longer given food after pecking the disk they continued to peck for a while but eventually gave up.

4. The time at which the reinforcement is given is very important. If the food is given immediately after the pigeon pecks the disk, he will continue to peck at a steady rate. In contrast, if there is a long delay between the pecking and the coming of the food, the reinforcement does not speed up the pigeon's performance. In other words, the shorter the time interval between the response and the reinforcement, the better the learning.

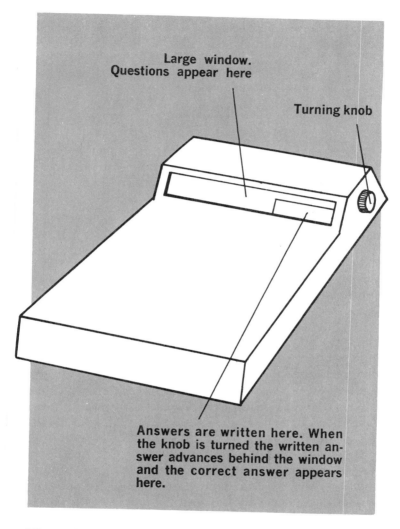

Large window. Questions appear here

Turning knob

Answers are written here. When the knob is turned the written answer advances behind the window and the correct answer appears here.

Figure 13-2. A Teaching Machine. The answers are written by the learner at the right of the window and the student turns a knob to see if he is correct.

ture where the hearer's attention might wander so that he misses significant facts, the teaching machine always has the learner's attention. When he daydreams or gets distracted the teaching machine stops until the learner returns to his task. Teachers are freed from lecturing and can help individual students who might be having difficulties with the subject matter.

It has been found that when teaching machines are not available it is possible to prepare special books which use the principles of reinforcement. The material is present in a form similar to that of figure 13-3 and the student completes the projects at home in his own time. In order to "get the feel" of programmed learning, the reader may want to take a pencil and complete the items of figure 13-3 before reading further.

By using programmed learning, both with and without machines, children have been taught spelling, grammar, reading, music, and such academic subjects as geography and history. Skinner has used machines to teach college courses in a number of subjects and more recently government, industry, the military, and some Sunday schools and seminaries have been making use of these new methods.

Teaching machines and programmed learning books are new and there is some reluctance to use them in Christian education. Perhaps some people feel that the use of these modern methods might in some way limit the power of the Holy Spirit. But the Holy Spirit can work through these techniques. Perhaps man has been permitted to discover an exciting and effective procedure for the teaching of Bible facts and the basics of theology.

Figure 13-3. — Part of a program to teach about the life and country of David. The machine presents one item at a time. The student completes the item and then turns the knob to expose the correct answer as shown on the right. To try this program, cover the column at the right. Do one item at a time. Fill in the blank first, and then uncover the answer.[3]

Sentence to be completed	Correct answer
1. Everyone remembers David. He was the shepherd boy who struck Goliath on the forehead with a stone from his sling. It was _____ who killed Goliath.	1. David
2. Perhaps you also remember that this shepherd boy grew up to become the Israelites' second king. The Israelites' second and most beloved king was _____.	2. David
3. When David became their king, the Israelites were living in what later came to be known as *Palestine*. To understand David we must learn about his people, called the _____ _____, and their country, called _____.	3. Israelites Palestine
4. Palestine is the name of the place where the Israelites lived. People called _____ occupied a land called _____.	4. Israelites Palestine
5. David became king of the _____ called Israelites. These people occupied the _____ of Palestine.	5. people land
6. Because many different people have lived there, Palestine has had many _____ names.	6. different (other, or equivalent)

7. When the Israelites came to Palestine they found people called Canaanites living there. The land was called the land of C - - - - n.

        7. (C) a n a a (n)

8. One of the early names for Palestine was the land of _____.

        8. Canaan

9. Later the Roman conquerors called the whole country P - - - - - - - -.

        9. (P) a l e s t i n e

10. The eastern Mediterranean washes against the coastal plains of Palestine. Therefore, Palestine is open to invasion by any nation which can cross the _____.

        10. Mediterranean Sea (eastern Mediterranean)

11. Just before David's time, the Philistines had come across the Mediterranean Sea and settled on the coastal plains of _____.

        11. Palestine

12. The Philistines were a seagoing people from Crete who occupied the _____ _____ of Palestine.

        12. coastal plains

13. The seafaring people who lived on the coastal plains of Palestine were called the Phil - - - - - - -.

        13. (Phil) i s t i n e s

14. In 1000 B.C.., the Israelites had to share Palestine with a seafaring people called the _____.

        14. Philistines

15. Palestine was open to invasion from the Mediterranean Sea. It was also used as a corridor by the large nations located north and south of it. The small country of Palestine had large nations lying _____ and _____ of it.

        15. north
           south

the learner should be understood in terms of the influences that have shaped his development.

11. **Anxiety** can influence learning. Mild anxiety sometimes helps learning and more intense anxiety almost always has a detrimental effect on learning.

12. The **incentives** to learn which may work for some learners may not work for others.

13. The learner's **values** are important. By this we mean that people are more likely to learn what they consider important than what they consider to be unimportant.

14. The **group atmosphere** of learning (whether there is competition or cooperation, whether the teacher is authoritative or democratic) will affect both the learning and the student's reaction to the learning situation.

Although most people consider education to be good and propaganda to be bad, such a distinction is not really justified. Both education and propaganda can be good at times, and both can be misused. If we are concerned about a non-believer's salvation, then giving him an unbiased lecture on world religion and leaving him to decide which to accept, if any, is education which is bad. If we are concerned about a child's teeth, then telling him to clean his teeth regularly is propaganda which is good. Jesus and other great preachers of the Bible were both educators and propagandists. In like manner, the church today must be involved in both Christian education and Christian propaganda.

Thus far in this chapter we have discussed techniques which are used primarily by the educator. Although many of these techniques — such as the use of teaching machines and programmed learning — could also be used by propagandists, the latter tend to use other procedures which have been found to be effective in causing people to change their opinions.

Effective Propaganda

Psychologists, sociologists, and experts in the field of speech have conducted several hundred experiments in an attempt to determine the ways in which opinions and attitudes can be changed in the direction desired by the propagandist. While this research is still going on, there are some facts about effective propaganda which are well established.[7]

First, it has been established that the reputation of the persuader has a direct bearing on whether or not the audience will accept the propaganda. Advertisers (who are almost always propagandists) frequently employ a well-known and highly respected movie star or athlete to speak in favor of a product. Drug manufacturers try to sell their medications by presenting the opinion of medical men because it is generally accepted that doctors are best prepared to give information about these products. It may be that the personal prestige of an evangelist like Billy Graham accounts for the greater number of people who come forward in his meetings than in those of his less famous associates.

The persuader's reputation is not enough to cause people to be influenced by propaganda. The listener is also affected by the motives which he attributes to the speaker. Although I know of no research in this area, we might suspect that few people are convinced when the tobacco industry presents evidence showing that cigarette smoking is *not* harmful to health. Obviously the cigarette manufacturers have a personal stake in how people react to smoking, and thus the listener is less likely to be swayed. In like manner, some people may resist the appeals of a preacher or religious leader because they are afraid that "he is out to convert me."

In addition to the prestige and motives attributed to persuaders, the intellectual abilities of the hearers and the influence of their friends are important. It has been found that people with high intelligence are more easily persuaded when presented with impressive logical arguments. They are less influenced when presented with illogical rambling speeches or with statements that have no basis in fact. Furthermore, people are more willing to accept propaganda if their friends accept it. From this we might conclude that young people are most often reached for Christ by other young people, and that professional men are best reached by other professionals.

The way in which the message is presented can also be significant. When an audience is friendly to the speaker, persuasive statements are likely to be accepted even though only one side of an argument is presented. More often, however, it is best to present both sides and to recognize that the issue presented last is the one which is most likely to stick. Strong threats are not very effective propaganda techniques nor is it usually wise to let your audience draw their own conclusions. Research shows that, in most cases, it is best to present reasons for one's opinions and to repeat the desired conclusion more than once.

The effect of the propaganda is likely to wear off in time but a good way to overcome this is to call for some kind of active response from the audience. During World War II an attempt was made to persuade housewives to serve kidneys to their families. The women who had listened to a lecture were uninfluenced by the propaganda but many of those who subsequently engaged in active discussion did change the family diet by serving more kidneys. Undoubtedly, this is one reason why coming to the front of an auditorium following an evangelistic service can bring about a greater change of behavior than encouraging a person to make a decision while remaining in his seat.

Unfortunately, it has also been discovered that the people whom the persuader would most like to influence are rarely in the audience. It is well known that few Democrats ever bother to attend a Republican rally and that there aren't very many Republicans at Democratic meetings. Probably few non-Christians ever listen to Christian radio programs. As a result speakers often find themselves trying to persuade an audience which is, for the most part, in agreement with the speaker already. This explains why few conversions occur in an evangelistic church service unless the unconverted person is invited to the service by a member of the church.

Resisting Propaganda

There are times when it is desirable for an individual to resist propaganda. After the Korean War it was recognized that soldiers could be trained to withstand the persuasive arguments of the enemy. Closer to the local church is the example of a college student who moves to a secular university campus where he is subjected, perhaps for the first time, to the arguments of those who are opposed to Christianity. Often these students are impressed and persuaded by anti-Christian propaganda since they fail to realize that there are good reasons for sticking with the Biblical faith.

Of course the simplest way to resist propaganda is to completely avoid hearing the contradictory points of view. This is probably one reason why people who have strong religious or political beliefs rarely pay much attention to the arguments of those with whom they disagree. This isolation makes people highly vulnerable when they are caught off guard and *forced* to hear the "other side" of an issue. Such is often the situation when a young Christian goes to a secular college and is unexpectedly presented with a position that is anti-Biblical.

Before discussing this further let us consider how a citizen of, let us say, Canada would avoid contracting typhoid fever. As long as he remains in Canada he is largely free from the threat of this disease. If he flies to the tropics and is forced by circumstances to drink some of the water, he would be vulnerable to infection. For this reason, the Canadian who plans to visit the tropics, where the danger of contracting typhoid fever is much greater than at home, would be immunized prior to his departure. By receiving a mild injection of typhoid bacteria, his body builds up resistance against possible future contact with this disease.

In like manner it is possible for people to be immunized against propaganda. Research has shown that people are most likely to be swayed by propaganda when the arguments are unexpected. If warned that they will be hearing arguments and ideas with which they may disagree, people are much less likely to be influenced into changing their opinions.[8] It has also been found that people who clearly know what they believe — and why — are more likely to cling to their beliefs than are those who do not specifically know the reasons for what they believe.[9] Perhaps the person who has made the effort to know what and why he believes is more committed to this position and thus less susceptible to opposing arguments.[10] An additional psychological finding is of special importance. The most effective way of building up resistance to persuasion is to present both sides of an issue and then to state both what is wrong with the opposition's belief and what is right about our position.[11] It is especially important to present both sides when dealing with people who are highly educated and intelligent.[12] Finally, research supports the common observation that people are less susceptible to persuasive communications if they have "allies" who believe as they do.[13]

These conclusions have direct practical application to Christian propaganda. Church members, especially teenagers who will be going to college, should be warned — by people whom they respect — that their beliefs will be questioned and criticized. Christians should be instructed in their faith so that they know what they believe and why.[14] Church members should be taught what the non-Christian believes, the reasons for these beliefs, and why Christians disagree. Finally, because of the importance of group support, Christians should be encouraged to seek fellowship with other Christians. Care should be taken not to let such fellowship become an excuse for isolation and withdrawal from the non-believing world. Such withdrawal is unbiblical.

Conclusions

To be effective, education must be concerned both with the present and with the future. The good teacher seeks to impart knowledge and develop skills in the learner which will be relevant in the present and helpful in the future. The professor in a medical school, for example, requires his students to learn facts about the structure and functioning of the human body, and about current treatment techniques. Students and teacher are both aware that medicine will change and that ten years after graduation the young doctor will be faced with new medical findings. The "keeping up to date" after graduation will be largely the doctor's own responsibility. For this reason the student must learn, even before he becomes a physician, how to keep abreast of latest developments and how to apply new techniques.

What is true of medical education, also applies to Bible teaching. The students must be instructed in scriptural truths. They must acquire Bible knowledge and apply it to their lives at present. But the world is changing and the teacher will not always be present. It is important that Bible students learn how to study on their own so that they will be able to independently search the scriptures. The writer of Hebrews was distressed because his readers had only been half educated. They were able to receive factual knowledge, but they had never learned how to teach themselves and others.[15]

When Jesus instructed his disciples to teach He did not say very much about the methodology to be used. The Holy Spirit is the one who really teaches us about spiritual things.[16] Under His guidance, we who are instructed to carry on a teaching ministry should use the most effective methodology known to man. The psychology of effective learning, teaching, education, and propaganda can be useful as we seek to fulfill this part of the great commission.

---

[1] *Much of this research is reported in* Roger Ulrich, Thomas Stachnik, *and* John Mabry, Control of Human Behavior. *Glenview, Illinois: Scott, Foresman and Company, 1966.*

[2] *For a concise summary of B. F. Skinner's work with pigeons and his view of teaching machines, see his book* The Technology of Teaching. *New York: Appleton - Century - Crofts, 1968.*

[3] *From David: A Bible Study by Theodor Mauch, prepared by the Department of Christian Education of the Executive Council of the Protestant Episcopal Church. Copyright © 1965 by The Seabury Press, Inc. Used by permission.*

[4] *The test answers are as follows:*
1. *David*
2. *Palestine*
3. *Canaan*
4. *Mediterranean Sea*

5. *Israelites, Philistines*

6. *Seafarers, Traders, Herdsmen, Soldiers.*

[5] *Adapted from Ernest R. Hilgard and Gordon H. Bower.* Theories of Learning *(Third edition). New York: Appleton - Century - Crofts, 1966, pp. 562-564. Copyright © 1966 by Meredith Corporation. Used by permission.*

[6] *The sermon on the Mount includes both education and propaganda. In Matthew 5:21-22; 27-28; 31-32; 33-37; 38-39; 43-45; 6:2-4; 5–8; 16-18. Jesus mixes education and propaganda. He presents both sides, but he encourages the people to choose one position. In the remainder of Matthew 6 and in most of Matthew 7 Jesus primarily presents propaganda.*

[7] *Much of the information contained in the following paragraphs is adapted from Herbert I. Abelson,* Persuasion: How Opinions and Attitudes are Changed. *New York: Springer, 1959.*

[8] *Jane Allyn and L. Festinger, "The Effectiveness of Unanticipated Persuasive Communications,"* Journal of Abnormal and Social Psychology, *1961, 62, pp. 35-40.* I. L. Janis and R. F. *Terwilliger, "An Experimental Study of Psychological Resistances to Fear Arousing Communications,"* Journal of Abnormal and Social Psychology, *1962, 65, pp. 403-410.*

[9] *E. H. Schein, I. Schneier, and C. H. Barker,* Coercive Persuasion, *New York: Norton, 1961, p. 168.*

[10] *R. R. Blake and Jane S. Mouton, "The Experimental Investigation of Interpersonal Influence," In A. D. Biderman and H. Zimmer (Editors),* The Manipulation of Human Behavior, *New York: Wiley, 1961, pp. 216-276.*

[11] *A. A. Lumsdaine and I. L. Janis. "Resistance to 'Counter-Propaganda' Produced by One-sided and Two-sided 'Propaganda' Presentations," In Eleanor E. Maccoby, T. M. Newcomb, and E. L. Hartley (Editors)* Readings in Social Psychology, *New York: Henry Holt, 1958, pp. 131-137. P. C. Lewan and E. Stotland, "The Effects of Prior Information on Susceptibility to an Emotional Appeal,"* Journal of Abnormal and Social Psychology, *1961, 62, pp. 450-453. W. J. McGuire, "Resistance to Persuasion Conferred by Active and Passive Prior Refutation of the Same and Alternative Counterarguments,"* Journal of Abnormal and Social Psychology, *1961, 63, pp. 326-332. W. J. McGuire, "Persistence of the Resistance to Persuasion Induced by Various*

Types of Prior Belief Defenses," Journal of Abnormal and Social Psychology, *1962, 64, pp. 241-248.*

[12] *C. I. Hovland, A. A. Lumsdaine and F. D. Sheffield, "The Effects of Presenting 'One Side' Versus 'Both Sides' in Changing Opinions on a Controversial Subject." In W. Schramm (Editor),* The Process and Effects of Mass Communication, *Urbana, Illinois: University of Illinois Press, 1961, pp. 261-274.*

[13] *Asch,* op. cit.

[14] *It is the author's opinion that few church members can state explicitly what they believe. As a demonstration of this, the reader might attempt to write out his own statement of faith —or invite the members of a Sunday school class to do this.*

[15] *Hebrews 5:11-14.*

[16] *Luke 12:12; John 14:26; I Corinthians 2:13; I John 2:27.*

14

PSYCHOLOGY IN THE LOCAL CHURCH

The science of psychology has been applied in many practical situations. Colleges and universities, clinics and hospitals, industrial institutions, governments, schools, prisons, businesses, advertising agencies, and military installations all make use of psychological knowledge and skills. Psychologists are involved in such varied activities as treating the mentally ill, selecting employees for industry, helping teenagers to decide on careers, mending broken marriages, conducting research to determine what signs are most easily seen along super-highways, designing instrument panels for airplanes, helping to rehabilitate prisoners, improving grade school teaching, giving intellifence tests to children, counseling with alcoholics, advising parents on how to bring up their children, designing effective advertisements, and studying such diverse problems as how brain tumors affect behavior or how people react when they don't get enough sleep. It should not be surprising that a science which has application to so many segments of society can also be of assistance in the work of the church. This chapter will consider five of the many areas where psychology can make such a contribution.

Understanding Normal Human Development

"Developmental psychology" is a branch of psychology which studies how normal people develop. It is well known that as people mature they experience physical changes which in turn influence behavior. Developmental psychology studies these physical and behavioral changes and considers the problems which most of us face as we go through life.

As an example, let us consider the period of adolescence. At the age of eleven or twelve (depending on the individual) rapid physical changes begin to occur. One of these changes is the "growth spurt." Within a short period of time the individual shoots up and develops an adult sized body which at the beginning is awkward, clumsy, and hard to handle. The teenager discovers that he looks like an adult and is expected to act like an adult, but he still thinks like a child, behaves like a child, and often expresses emotion like a child. As he matures sexually, the adolescent experiences new urges which he must learn to control. Other physical changes, such as the growth of beards in the male, the development of breasts in the female, and changes in the body proportions and tone of voice in both sexes, can cause considerable tension in the adolescent. He discovers, that physical changes can be embarrassing. There is nothing more humiliating for a young teenager than to have his voice crack or to have someone tease him about the fuzz that is just appearing on his face.

While adjusting to these physical changes, the normal adolescent is also learning to develop independence and to rely less on his parents. This is not easy and often the teenager will associate with other young people of about the same age who are having similar problems in breaking away from home. Group solidarity becomes important as emphasized by such things as outlandish (from the adult point of view) clothing, unusual hairstyles, slang which nobody over twenty-five can understand, teenage music (or noise depending on your point of view) and a number of tribal dances. Many times as adolescents throw over childish ways and learn how to be adults they begin to question and sometimes reject the religious beliefs that they have been taught as children in Sunday School or in the home.

Parents and other adults, might not agree with the thinking of the teenager or with the way in which he dresses, amuses himself, or cuts his hair. Nevertheless, the church can have a more effective ministry with these young people if we recognize the physical and psychological conflicts which every normal adolescent encounters. Psychologists have carefully studied this period of life and can assist the church member to better understand and deal with the teenage behavior.

At the other end of life, the physical changes and frustrations of old people have also been studied by psychologists. In the United States there are about eighteen million people over sixty-five. Every year this age group has a net increase of more than four hundred thousand people. For many these are not "golden years." Instead, they are years of loneliness and physical hardship. Widowhood, loss of friends and relatives, physical decline, feelings of uselessness, and financial problems combine to cause considerable difficulties for many people in their later years. Where he worships the old person often feels unwanted and left out because the church, like our whole society, is much more interested in young people and youth programs. It is not difficult to understand why old people sometimes complain, dwell in the past, or seek to associate with those who are younger. With increased understanding of the older person's problems, the church could minister to this group much more effectively. Psychologists have studied every age period from the time of conception to the time of death. For pastors and congregations who are familiar with some of these findings, psychology can make a considerable contribution to the ministry of the church.

Understanding Abnormal Behavior

It is easy to jump to conclusions about the cause of mental illness. As we have seen in chapter five, abnormal behavior is very complex and its causes are numerous. To conclude that a mental illness results because someone is "spiritually dead" or because he "had a bad background" is vague, naive, and overly simplified.

Since a number of psychologists have spent their lives in the study of abnormal behavior, the church could benefit from the insight and understanding of these men. By developing a greater appreciation for the complex causes of abnormality we can have greater patience and understanding in dealing with people who have problems.

Promoting Psychological Stability

In the late 1950s the University of Michigan Research Center conducted a survey in which hundreds of people were asked if they had ever had a problem for which professional help would have been useful. One out of four of the respondents replied "yes," and of these, one out of seven reported that they had actually sought help. It is interesting to note that of the people who talked to some professional counselor, only ten per cent went to psychiatrists, psychologists, or other private practitioners. Twenty-nine had seen their local physician and an amazing forty-two per cent reported that they had gone to their pastor or clergyman.[1]

Whether they are trained for this or not, pastors and other church leaders are involved in counseling — the art of helping people to handle their problems and efficiently meet the stresses of society. There are at least two reasons why church leaders will continue to be counselors. First, the church does not charge for counseling services. Secondly, there are not enough professional resources in our communities to handle all of the counseling problems. Psychiatrists and psychologists are scarce and there are not enough to go around. Psychology can make a great contribution therefore in the training of ministers, Sunday school teachers, and other Christians who will be called upon to do counseling. A number of useful books, some authored by psychologists, have been written to help the church leader develop these counseling skills.[2]

Training in the art of counseling is not the only area where psychology can assist church leaders as they help people to get along better. The prevention of problems may be even more important than the solving of problems. Premarital discussion groups or classes, preaching that deals with personal needs (such preaching can be quite consistent with the Word of God), activities in the church which are family-centered so that they strengthen rather than divide the family unit, carefully planned Sunday school programs, reverent worship services, small group discussions, prayer meetings, and Bible study groups, can all contribute to the greater psychological stability of people in the church. Psychology could show church leaders how these and other techniques can contribute to the well being of church members.[3]

We must remember that laymen are not the only

people in the church who encounter problems. Pastors and their families are in a demanding work which is often characterized by intense pressure.[4] The pastor has a lonely job. He and his wife must listen to the problems of others — for this is an important part of their ministry — but there are few human ears to whom they can confidentially express their own discouragements and frustrations. Frequently there is financial strain because of the low salaries in the ministry. At the same time the pastor is expected to dress well, maintain a nice home, and entertain frequently. In addition, the pastor must fulfill many roles: administrator, preacher, evangelist, youth leader, janitor, scholar, father, husband, counselor, budget director, parish promoter, and community problem solver, to name a few. His wife, who often has had little or no theological training, is sometimes expected to speak, make calls, attend all meetings and generally fulfill the functions of assistant pastor. Even the pastor's children are under pressure to be models of good behavior, strongly spiritual, and present at all meetings of their age group. Little wonder that "preacher's kids" are sometimes poorly adjusted. All of these demands can rob the pastor and his family of necessary time with God, interfere with family life, and bring about feelings of anxiety, discouragement, and inferiority when there is criticism or when things are not running smoothly. What is most pathetic about this is that many of the pastor's pressures come from well meaning but critical and inconsiderate church members. Perhaps better than anyone else, the psychologist can remind the church member to be more sensitive to the pressures of the ministry and to do whatever he can to contribute to the mental stability of the pastor and his family.

Conducting Research

Church leaders are usually very busy people. It is the height of ineffiency, however, to spend a great deal of time, much effort, and a lot of the Lord's money designing well thought-out and well planned Christian education programs, Sunday school meetings, youth projects, radio programs, advertising campaigns, and other activities, without ever stopping to systematically evaluate what we have been doing. Psychologists have spent a great deal of time designing and testing techniques which enable us to measure and study human behavior. Some of these techniques could be used in evaluating the work of the local church.

In discussing research in the church we recognize that the ultimate value of church work is determined by God. The scriptures teach that the Word of God will go forth and prosper.[5] Psychological research tools will never be adequate to study the moving of God's Spirit.[6] With the full recognition of this truth, however, it is still wise to evaluate some of the things which are done in the church.

As an example of the value of research, consider the field of advertising. Suppose that a business man wants to know how he can effectively advertise his product. He might go to different areas of the country and check sales. Let us assume that he finds sales to be about the same in area A and area B. Then he puts on an advertising campaign. Area A is exposed to a number of television commercials. Area B does not get any television coverage. Then the business man checks again to see if there has been a change in buying behavior following the advertising campaign. If the television commercials were successful, obviously people in area A will purchase more of the product than will the people in area B. Research into human buying behavior has shown that advertising works and that some kinds of advertising are more effective than others.

A drug manufacturer might use some of the same techniques. Before putting the drug on the market he must be sure that it is effective. To find this out he might take two groups of people — group X and group Y. At the beginning, all participants might be given a physical examination to make sure that they are equally healthy. Then let us give the drug to group X. Group Y will not get the drug. Since the very act of taking a pill can have a psychological effect which could influence the results, group Y will take a "sugar pill" that looks like the drug. The participants in this experiment should not know whether they are getting the drug or the sugar pill. After group X gets the drug and group Y does not we will test the effect of the medication. Suppose both groups are exposed to a disease. (Perhaps both groups live in an area where a flu epidemic or other disease is prevalent. If it is a serious disease the experimenter would work with animals first, before giving the drug to people.) Suppose that the people in group X, which has had the drug, do not develop the disease. In contrast, those in group Y, develop the disease. From this we could conclude that probably the drug is doing the work of immunizing people in group X against the disease.

The church can use research techniques similar to these. In working with high school students we might want the young people to develop certain attitudes and behavior. Perhaps we want them to see the importance of daily devotions so that they come to spend time each day in prayer and Bible study. To determine the most effective way of stimulating such behavior, we might send a questionnaire to all of the young people to find out to what extent they are now spending time in daily devotions.[7] Then, we might select two groups with similar devotional habits. With group X we might have a discussion on the value of devotions. We allow the students to chat about the topic. To group Y we give a lecture entitled "Why you should have devotions." Later we will ask again to determine if any change has taken place in the reported behavior of the students. Have they changed in their attitudes and behavior as a result of our Christian education program on the value of devotions? Has the lecture been more effective than the discussion method? Such a study could indicate if any change occurred at all and which method of instruction was more valuable.

While there are problems in applying research techniques to the Lord's work, a greater use of research methodology undoubtedly could be used to increase efficiency of local church work.

Understanding How Psychology, Scripture, and the Church are Related

The whole purpose of this book has been to show how psychology can be related to Christianity. There are at least three reasons why church members should have some understanding of the relationships between psychology, the Bible, and the work of the church.

First, psychology can help us to understand human behavior. Such understanding enables Christians to appreciate the causes and symptoms of abnormal behavior, helps us to understand human nature and the occurrence of miracles, sheds light on the nature of conversion, shows how some people use Christianity as a crutch, alerts us to neurotic behavior that could interfere with the Lord's work and shows us how preaching can deviate from the Word of God and rely instead on psychological gimmicks. In short, a familiarization with psychology can increase our appreciation for and understanding of both the world around us and the Word of God.

Secondly, many people who criticize the Bible and the church base their criticisms on psychological arguments. A knowledge of these arguments enables us to answer the critics and to show them that the Word of God stands firm in spite of psychological criticisms.

Thirdly, an understanding of psychology can have practical value. If we understand the psychological principles of counseling, the ways in which people learn, the principles of propaganda, and the techniques of psychological research, our work in the local church might be much more efficient.

In Conclusion: A Warning!

Psychology can be of value in the work of the church, but let us never become so impressed with this science that it becomes an idol and the basis of our whole church program. There is a danger lest church people learn a little psychology and begin to act as though they were competent psychologists. Pastors can become so involved in counseling that they have no time for Bible study, prayer or the preparation of messages. Sermons and Sunday school lessons can degenerate into discourses on how to be well-adjusted and the Word of God can be eliminated except for verses here and there which, whether quoted out of context or not, might be of assistance in supporting the psychological point that the speaker is trying to get across. Prayer meetings can cease to be prayer meetings and become small group therapy sessions instead. Seminaries can reduce course offerings in theology and Bible in order that the students can spend more time studying psychology and counseling. This over acceptance of psychology has ruined the witness of many churches and seminaries. They have neglected their original calling, turned from Christ and the scriptures, and become shrines to the modern science of psychology.

It must always be remembered that psychology is a *tool* of the church and must never become the *work* of the church. It is the Holy Spirit, who convicts men of sin. The Holy Spirit and the Bible teach men and enable them to grow spiritually. In His work the Holy Spirit can and does use tools. Modern psychology might be one of these tools. If evangelicals carefully avoid over dependence on psychology, then this exciting science of behavior can be a valuable aid both in our understanding of each other and in the work to which we have been called by God.

[1] *Joint Commission on Mental Illness and Health,* Action for Mental Health. *New York, Science Editions, Inc., 1961.*

[2] *One such book is by John W. Drakeford,* Counseling for Church Leaders. *Nashville, Tennessee: Broadman, 1961. See also R. May,* The Art of Counseling, *New York: Abingdon, 1939.*

[3] *Although the theology is liberal, the psychology is good in Howard J. Clinebell, Jr.,* Mental Health Through Christian Community: The Local Church's Ministry of Growth and Health. *New York: Abingdon, 1965.*

[4] *Much of the following discussion is adapted from Gary R. Collins, Mental Health in the Ministry,* The Pastor's Manual, *Fall, 1965, pp. 2-7.*

[5] *Isaiah 55:11.*

[6] *John 3:8.*

[7] *We cannot assume that the questionnaires will always be answered honestly. There are ways of encouraging and checking this, but a description of such techniques is beyond the scope of this discussion.*

INDEX